# BOMBS OVER DUBLIN

BOMBS OVER DUBLIN

SEAN MCMAHON

CURRACH
PRESS

## ACKNOWLEDGEMENTS

My thanks are due to Richard Doherty, Brian McMahon and especially Jo O'Donoghue of Currach Press, the best of editors and collaborators.

First published in 2009 by
CURRACH PRESS
55A Spruce Avenue, Stillorgan Industrial Park, Blackrock, Co. Dublin
www.currach.ie
1 3 5 4 2
Cover by bluett
Origination by Currach Press
Printed in Ireland by ColourBooks, Baldoyle Industrial Estate, Dublin 13
ISBN:978-1-85607-983-9

# Contents

# DRAMATIS PERSONAE

Frank Aiken (1898–1983), who had been an IRA leader in the War of Independence, was a founder member of Fianna Fáil in 1926 and was minister in all the governments formed by that party from 1932, holding the portfolio of Defence (1932–9) and the important post of Minister for Coordination of Defensive Measures during the Second World War and serving as Minister for External Affairs (1951–4; 1957–69).

Sir Winston Churchill (1874–1965) was execrated in Ireland for his refusal in 1920 to recognise the IRA as a legitimate army at war and for imposing the Auxiliaries as a terror force. He took part in the Treaty negotiations and strongly supported the Free State. He bitterly resented the return of the Treaty ports to Éire and as British Prime Minister in the Second World War continued to agitate for their return to Allied control. His appointment of Sir John Maffey as British minister to Éire was unusually far-sighted.

Éamon de Valera (1882–1975), the only surviving leader of the Easter Rising, became leader of the Fianna Fáil in 1926 and was Taoiseach from 1933. When it became clear that a war in Europe was imminent, he asserted as Taoiseach and Minister for Foreign Affairs that Éire would remain neutral. This stance he maintained, often with great difficulty, against persuasion amounting to bullying by both Britain and America.

David Gray (1870–1968) was the uncle by marriage of Eleanor Roosevelt, the wife of the American president Franklin Delano Roosevelt. He was appointed American representative in Éire (1940–49) at the age of seventy and for all his tenure was at odds with the Irish government and especially with de Valera, whom he wrongly accused of favouring Germany. De Valera continually requested his recall even after Roosevelt's death but his successor Harry S. Truman (1884–1972) allowed him to stay until his eightieth year, with the result that diplomatic relations between Éire and the US were no better for the coalition government that succeeded Fianna Fáil.

Eduard Hempel (1887–1972) was representative of Nazi Germany in Éire (1937–45). De Valera had specifically requested that the envoy should not be a member of the Nazi party but Hempel was forced to join party the year after his appointment. Relations between de Valera and Hempel were quite friendly – to the dismay of Gray – but the charges of espionage made by Gray against Hempel were without foundation.

Sir John Loader Maffey, 1st Baron Rugby (1877–1969), served as British minister to Éire (1939–49). He liked Ireland and was on friendly terms with de Valera, probably aware that his much-publicised neutrality secretly favoured the Allies. Their good relations eased tensions between the two countries, in notable contrast with David Gray, the American representative.

# 1

## 'Neutral Island'

One of the greatest tests that the state of southern Ireland had to face in the twenty years since its inception in 1922 was the vexed question of its neutrality during the Second World War. Under the terms of the 1937 constitution the politically inaccurate designation 'Éire' replaced the accurate but unsatisfactory 'Free State' – *Saorstát Éireann*, if you insisted. At first the term pleased no one except Northern Unionists, who used it as a means of distancing themselves from the separated brethren, and the postage stamp designers who did and still do a very artistic job and found the four-letter word amenable to incorporation in their designs. Its convenience eventually seemed to outweigh its difficulties for use in the acquiescent south and it became the standard term of reference for the twenty-six quasi-independent counties from then on. It also symbolised nationalist aspiration to an ultimately integral country.

The threat of a European war came hard upon the peace settlement of Éire's own 'Economic War' with Britain. That conflict had not long been finished, its terms including the vexatious Irish custody of the retained Treaty ports, and the bloodless battles had been replaced by a wary amity. Some reasonable people were even prepared to admit that Malcolm MacDonald (1901–81), Secretary of State for the Colonies from 1934, had shown exemplary patience on the British side during the protracted negotiations.

Almost immediately after the invasion of Poland by the *Wehrmacht*, Éire was placed, or put itself, under emergency footing. The more extreme elements of the population – notably the residual IRA who were still instinctively fighting the civil war, the cessation of which many had not approved of – became vociferously pro-German and said so publicly. Many others assented to this view privately, no doubt reprising the old mantra: 'England's difficulty; Ireland's opportunity.'

Éamon de Valera (1882–1975) had been Taoiseach for seven years by 1939 and also took charge of foreign affairs. For a while during what was with hindsight called the 'phoney war' the Irish army was mobilised and many amateur (but efficient) sailors joined the navy. They did not, as in the Irving Berlin song of the time, see the world – nor did they see much of the sea.

The number of regular soldiers in the army was about 7500, of whom 630 were commissioned officers and 1500 were NCOs. They were well trained and as efficient as those of any comparative small country but under-equipped. The reserve units had about 200 officers and 5000 other ranks and when the voluntary part-timers were added the total of trained and partly trained reached 20,000. The Irish Marine Service, established in November 1939, maintained two fishery-protection vessels and had six motor-torpedo boats on order but not yet delivered from Britain, while the Air Corps strength was virtually nil. In fact there were only sixteen serviceable planes, four of them fighters, all surely obsolescent if not actually obsolete. There was little in the way of anti-aircraft artillery and no searchlights.

De Valera was emphatic about the need for Ireland to remain for as long as possible out of the conflict that would affect most of the rest of the world. As he stated in an interview in the London *Evening Standard* as early as 13 October 1938: 'We have definitely committed ourselves to the proposition that this island shall not be used as a base for enemy attacks upon Britain.'

On 2 September 1939, the day before war was declared by Britain, an announcement of the state of emergency was made in the Dáil:

> Arising out of the armed conflict now taking place in Europe, a national emergency exists affecting the vital interests of the State.

De Valera in his customary, paternalistic way had some admonitory things to say on the same occasion:

> It is not as representing the sentiments or feelings of our people that the government stands before you with this policy. It stands before you as the guardian of the interests of our people, and it is to guard those interests as best we can that we are proposing to follow the policy.

He reiterated the position later that same month:

> I have stated in this house, and I have stated in the country, that the aim of government policy is

to keep this country out of the war, and nobody, either here or elsewhere, has any right to assume anything else.

The great majority of the people of Éire approved of this stance, and all members of the Dáil with the notable exception of Fine Gael's James Dillon (1902–86), who wished to ally Éire with Britain. He was expelled from Fine Gael as a result of this continued public stance but lived on to have a full political career as an independent and to become leader of the Fine Gael party again in 1959.

Éire was at the time in the same position as Belgium, Holland Luxembourg, Denmark, Norway, Sweden, Finland, Hungary, Yugoslavia, Romania, Bulgaria, Portugal, Switzerland and Italy, that is to say, non-combatant. The United States, too, in spite of the openness of its president Franklin Delano Roosevelt (1882–1945), were and hoped to remain isolated from any European conflict. By 1942 only Sweden, Portugal, Spain and Éire of these countries had been allowed to stay neutral. Their detachment from the great cataclysm was not quite pure, however: Sweden was a covert appeaser of Germany; Spain and Portugal were convenient if unwilling hotbeds of espionage; Switzerland was a refuge for escaped POWs, if you can believe the war movies; and Éire, as will become clear, though it undoubtedly remained neutral, tended, without being anti-Axis, to be more lenient towards the Allies. This mildly pro-British stance was itemised by Viscount Cranbourne, later 5th Marquis of Salisbury (1893–1972), no friend of Ireland, as follows:

a.  They agreed to our use of Lough Foyle for naval and
    air purposes. The ownership of the Lough is disputed
    but the Southern Irish authorities are tacitly not
    pressing their claim in present conditions and are also
    ignoring any flying over the Donegal shore of the
    Lough, which is necessary in certain wind conditions
    to enable flying boats to take off from the Lough.

b.  They have agreed the use by our aircraft based on
    Lough Erne of a corridor over Southern Irish territory
    [known as the Donegal corridor] and territorial
    waters [then defined as three miles from shore] for
    the purpose of flying out to the Atlantic.

c.  They have arranged for the immediate transmission
    of the United Kingdom Representative's Office in
    Dublin of reports of submarine activity received from
    their coast watching service.

d.  They arranged for the broadcasting of reports by
    their Air Observer Corps of aircraft sighted over or
    approaching Southern Irish territory. (This does not
    include our aircraft using the corridor referred to in
    (b) above.)

e.  They arranged for the extinction of trade and business
    lighting in coastal towns where such lighting was
    alleged to afford a useful landmark for German
    aircraft.

f.  They have continued to supply us with meteorological
    reports.

g.  They have agreed to the use by our ships and aircraft
    of two wireless direction-finding stations at Malin
    Head.

h.  They have supplied particulars of German crashed

aircraft and personnel crashed or washed ashore or arrested on land.

i.   They arranged for staff talks on the question of co-operation against a possible German invasion of Southern Ireland, and close contact has since been maintained between the respective military authorities.

j.   They continue to intern all German fighting personnel reaching Southern Ireland. On the other hand, though, after protracted negotiations, Allied service personnel are now allowed to depart freely and full assistance is given in recovering damaged aircraft

k.   Recently, in connection with the establishment of prisoner of war camps in Northern Ireland, they have agreed either to return or at least intern any German prisoners who may escape from Northern Ireland across the border into Southern Ireland.

l.   They have, though, offered no objection to the departure from Southern Ireland of persons wishing to serve in the United Kingdom Forces nor to the journey on leave of such persons to and from Southern Ireland (in plain clothes).

m.   They have continued to exchange information with our security authorities regarding all aliens (including Germans) in Southern Ireland.

n.   They have (within the last few days) agreed to our establishing a Radar Station for use against the latest form of submarine activity.

Cranbourne afterwards admitted that the Irish government was 'willing to accord to us any facilities which would not be regarded as overtly prejudicing their attitude to neutrality'. These details emerged only later and it was really to the advantage of both countries that the true details of the exact nature of Éire's neutrality remained secret.

The majority of ordinary British (and Irish) citizens believed that Éire's stance in the matter was absolute. The result was that many on both sides of the Irish Sea believed than the country was full of Nazi spies. Members of the residual IRA were courted as spies and willing to behave as such but they proved to be of little consequence. In fact G2, the anti-espionage department led by Colonel Dan Bryan (1900–85), a man with much intelligence experience, was extremely efficient. Sir John Maffey (1877–1969), who had been appointed United Kingdom representative in Dublin in September 1939, was full of praise for that department, noting their 'rigid surveillance of the German Legation, the impounding of their wireless transmitter and close understanding with the British Intelligence Service. In this underground of espionage and intrigue a British authority in Ireland could never achieve what was achieved by native authority: "The dog of the country hunts the hare of the country."'

An example of the close watch kept on likely subversives was the discovery by the Garda Síochána in May 1940 of details of 'Plan Kathleen' in the home in County Wicklow of Iseult Stuart (1894–1954), wife of the absent writer Francis Stuart (1902–2000) and daughter of Maud Gonne (1865–1953). It was a plan devised by the IRA which suggested that they should attack across the border from the south to meet German paratroops dropped at Divis Mountain near Belfast and Lisburn, while commandos should land at

Lough Swilly and sweep across Lough Foyle from Moville to land at Magilligan Point. The attack would have netted Belfast and Derry and the occupation of the rest of Northern Ireland would therefore have been easy. In fact the plan had little chance of success even if Germany had the resources to implement it. The authorities in Berlin never considered it seriously and it was shelved. Twenty-four hours after the discovery of these plans photostats were in the hands of MI5 in London, who passed them on to the RUC in Belfast. It was decided that they were not required to take any action. With calculated irony the same scenario was used as the basis of a war game by the British army the following year.

One reason for de Valera's softness towards the Allies was his clear understanding, through his years with the League of Nations, of the true nature of Hitler's ambitions and the reality of Nazism. Another may have been the fact that up to 50,000 Éire citizens had joined the British armed services. The insistence on the right to declare and implement neutrality was a function of the national sovereignty that de Valera intended to claim eventually. A reminder that this absolute sovereignty had not been yet recognised by Britain was the naming of Maffey as 'Representative' and not the full title of 'Ambassador'. Time and again, too, de Valera insisted that the business of sovereignty and neutrality was inextricably linked with that of partition. He was logical and unhelpful enough to express outrage after Pearl Harbor at the presence of US forces on Irish territory without his government's permission; Irish territory for him included the north.

In this he was joined by the fiery Cardinal Joseph MacRory (1861–1945) who had been Bishop of Down and Connor during the anti-Catholic pogrom in Belfast and elsewhere that heralded the coming into existence of the Northern Ireland state. Cardinal MacRory issued a statement on 27 September 1942 condemning the arrival of the GIs:

> When I read day after day in the press that this war is being fought for the rights and liberties of small nations and then think of my own corner of my country overrun by British and United States soldiers against the will of the nation I confess I sometimes find it hard to be patient.

He was equally vocal in expressing in the name of the whole of nationalist Ireland, as he had the right to do as the primate, the rejection of conscription as urged by the Unionist government in Stormont. This suggestion was not welcomed by the British government as they considered it likely to cause further trouble in Ulster (a view shared, if unexpressed, by many Unionists) so that Winston Churchill (1874–1965), the British premier, had to tell Lord Craigavon (1871–1941), the Northern Ireland prime minister, on 27 May 1941 that 'It would be more trouble than it was worth to enforce.'

De Valera proved adamantine even in answer to the offer by Malcolm MacDonald on 21 June 1940 of a united Ireland in principle in return for use of Éire territory, including the Treaty ports. His words, 'There should be a declaration of a united Ireland in principle; the constitutional and other practical details of the union to be worked out in due course...', though meant sincerely showed little awareness of the unyielding nature of Unionist attitudes. De Valera greatly admired MacDonald but he was under no illusion about the vagueness of the offer and the inability of the British government to deliver. His only offer in response, hardly acceptable, was stated that same day:

> That Éire and Ulster should be merged in a united Ireland, which should at once be neutral; its neutrality to be guaranteed by Great Britain and the United States of America; since Britain was a belligerent its military and naval forces should not take any active part in guaranteeing that neutrality but American ships should come into the Irish ports, and perhaps American troops into Ireland, to effect this guarantee.

At a meeting with de Valera four days later, MacDonald said that if Éire had come into the war it was 'unthinkable that the promise should be broken'. There the question of neutrality rested for the time being but it was to recur again from time to time.

One important aspect of the powers assumed by the government under the terms of the declaration of the emergency was the strict censorship of any slight element of pro-Britishness in books, films and broadcasts. (They were equally determined not to seem to support the Reich.) One example of the lengths to which the stringent rules went was evident in the case of the innocuous series of Sherlock Holmes films made usually about three a year by Universal Studios with what many (including me) regard as the best ever Holmes and Watson, Basil Rathbone (1892–1967) and Nigel Bruce (1895-1953). The partnership had begun with *The Hound of the Baskervilles* (1939) made by 20th-Century Fox before the war began and it was followed by *The Adventures of Sherlock*

*Holmes* that same year. Both were correctly set in the 1890s and shown freely in Éire but when Universal Studios decided to maintain the popular series and make them contemporary (with Holmes wearing a tweed hat instead of a deerstalker) they ran into censorship trouble. *The Voice of Terror* (1942), *The Secret Weapon* (1942) and *Sherlock Holmes in Washington* (1943) showed the pair of sleuths fighting the Nazis as decent Britishers should and as such could not be shown in Éire. The first of the dozen films made by Universal that was permitted to be shown in Dublin and elsewhere was *The Scarlet Claw* (1944); it was set safely in Canada and free from 'propaganda'.

'Propaganda' films were easily defined as ones about the war in which gallant Allied soldiers beat the Germans or realistically were more often defeated. The situation worsened after Pearl Harbor with the Japanese as a new enemy, when these islands were saturated with such films as *The First of the Few* (1942), *The Foreman Went to France* (1942), *Five Graves to Cairo* (1943), *Wake Island* (1943), *Guadalcanal Diary* (1943) and *Bataan* (1943). It must be admitted that the extensive nationalist cinema population in Northern Ireland called these films 'propaganda' too but enjoyed them just the same.

The effect of this cocooning of Éire made it easy for the population to accept that their neutral stance was not just a necessary one but the only moral one in the circumstances. They accepted the wartime shortages of white flour, petrol, tea, non-native fruits like oranges and bananas and rejoiced in the plenitude of liquor, meat and dairy products, when they could afford them. The poorer people, for whom bread and tea were a large part of their subsistence diet, felt the scarcities keenly. Along the border regions there was a twin flow of smuggling in opposite directions, immorally re-establishing a kind of dietary norm; the black market flourished. Visitors to Dublin were startled by the bright lights of shops and street lamps, the thickness of the steaks and the inexhaustible supply of Guinness, Jameson, Powers and whatever you're having yourself. *Dublin Opinion*, the humorous magazine that helped ease the wartime gloom, commented freely on such things as the ration of a half-ounce of tea per person per week. One number portrayed a perplexed housewife as the Wizard of half-Oz, a reference to one of the films that was not banned. The children, those unacknowledged but instinctive sociologists, sang in their skipping games:

*Here's to Lemass and old Sean MacEntee*
*With their dirty brown loaf and their half-ounce of tea.*

Sean Lemass (1899–1971) had the thankless post of Minister of Supplies, while MacEntee (1889–1984), old enough to the children in his early fifties but living to be much older, was Minister of Finance and later of Health.

Both the British and the Irish people assumed that the position of neutrality was absolute. Neither had any way of knowing just how relative the Irish government's position was. At the beginning the Chamberlain government was at least privately unconcerned. Lord Halifax (1891–1959), the Foreign Secretary, made the unpopular statement: 'British safety is not decreased but immeasurably increased by a free and friendly Ireland.' His successor, Anthony Eden (1897–1977), was also conciliatory. It was Winston Churchill who became and remained Ireland's greatest critic. As early as 5 May 1938 he showed his bitter disapproval of the handing back of the Treaty ports of Cobh, Berehaven and Lough Swilly. Speaking in the House of Commons, he described them with his customary rhetorical flourish as 'the sentinel towers of the western approaches, by which forty million people in this island so enormously depend for foreign food for their daily bread.'

Churchill laboured under the delusion that because he had read a deal of romantic Irish history and had spent some years in Ireland as a child when his grandfather was Viceroy, he knew the country better than other British politicians. He was execrated in Ireland, as he was for different reasons in the Welsh valleys, as the man who invented the Auxiliaries, the murderous force who made the grisly Black and Tans seem like boy scouts. After Churchill became prime minister, in May 1940, some of his brilliant rhetoric was directed against de Valera and the 'safe' Irish in their neutrality. On 5 November 1940, then prime minister for six months, he returned to the theme in the Commons:

> The fact that we cannot use the south and west coasts of Ireland to refuel our flotillas and aircraft, and thus protect the trade by which Ireland as well as Great Britain lives, is a most heavy and grievous burden and one which should never have been placed on our shoulders, broad though they may be.

The rhetoric was infectious: even so tolerant an Anglo-Irishman as Louis MacNeice (1907–63) could bring himself to snarl at the 'neutral island' in his poem 'Neutrality' and conclude it with the words:

> *While to the west of your own shores, the mackerel*
> *Are fat – on the flesh of your kin.*

Nicholas Monsarrat in *The Cruel Sea* (1951), his popular novel about British convoys in the north Atlantic, talked about the 'smug coastline' of Éire, 'past people who did not give a damn how long the war lasted as long as they could live on in their fairy tale world'. The cartoonists in the British press, largely to please their readership, showed U-boats plying freely in the Atlantic south of Ireland and, as with all pieces of propaganda, many even in Ireland believed in the strategic necessity of the ports. The denial of the use of the ports to the Royal Navy was stated by the Admiralty to have cost 368 ships and 5070 lives. It is not clear how the sea lords arrived at this figure. Truth is usually sacrificed to expediency in times of national danger and most historians would now agree that the significance of the ports in the war was less than politicians' rhetoric might have suggested.

The ports had certainly become an *idée fixe* with Churchill, a man notoriously prone to such fugues. Neville Chamberlain (1869–1940), Churchill's predecessor as prime minister, was not at all convinced of the necessity of clawing them back but he was ill, in the last year of his life, and suffered along with Halifax the reputation of being a 'Munich appeaser'. A glance at a map will make it clear that Lough Foyle is less tidal than Lough Swilly and was equally viable as a naval base (or as vulnerable to air attacks) as the previous inlet to the west. The virtues that had made Cobh in the south and Berehaven to the west safe refuges in the past from the long-distance guns of enemy battleships were meaningless when Stukas and Heinkels could penetrate right to the hearts of the bases. The further distances in nautical miles from Cork to Milford Haven, or Buncrana to Derry or the Scottish ports were not significant. In fact as was pointed out to David Gray (1870–1968), the American Ambassador, a persistent troublemaker and thorn in de Valera's side, the usual convoy route was round the north of Malin Head to Derry anyway. Anthony Eden, who replaced Halifax as Foreign Secretary, understood this as did Sir John Maffey, but Churchill, finding his self-fulfilling prophecy seeming to take place, regarded de Valera's and Éire's stance as a kind of personal insult. His quasi-hysterical telegram to de Valera on 8 December 1941:

> Now is your chance. Now or never. 'A nation once again'. Am very ready to meet you at any time.

was deliberately obscure and de Valera correctly ignored it. De Valera had always insisted that the return of the six counties of Northern Ireland and the full integrity of the Irish nation must be a prelude to allowing use of the ports.

The immediate effect of the declaration of emergency was the mobilising of the Irish army. A significant part of the personal equipment of any soldier in those years was the steel helmet. The model chosen by the Cumann na nGaedheal government in 1928 was the 'Vickers' that replicated the German Great War *Stahlhelm*. Because of the insistence of the Treaty of Versailles on a disarmed Germany there were then no factories to fulfil the defence forces' order and the firm of Vickers Ltd of London accepted the order for 5000 helmets, using German machinery. They were painted dark-green but in the days of black-and-white photography they look ominously like the *Wehrmacht* that cinema newsreels had shown marching into Austria, Czechoslovakia and, most recently, Poland. It became the habit of the British media, especially in newsreels, to show just how much like the hated Germans these neutral Éire soldiers were. Some Irish people were not ready to relinquish Britain as the enemy – one old farmer admitted to a reporter that he would like to see the English 'nearly bate' – and there were a few diehards who would have been prepared to form a fifth column of Nazi supporters. (This same group afterwards insisted that the horrifying pictures from Auschwitz, Dachau and Belsen were yet more examples of British propaganda and that the bombs that fell on various parts of the neutral country were dropped by RAF bombers. When the bombs were proved to be German they were certain that they were *captured* German bombs dropped by British planes.) The Vickers helmets were replaced in 1940 when the decent lads of the army were given helmets that made them look like British Tommies, which for some was even worse.

At home in Ireland a majority were more than half-content not to be involved in a second frightful world war a mere twenty-one years after the 'war to end all wars' had been concluded. They saw how Holland, Belgium, Norway, Finland and all the Balkan states had war thrust upon them and often wondered how it was that they escaped and were not invaded either by the Germans or from Northern Ireland by the British. By then they knew which they preferred. Another *Dublin Opinion* cartoon by Charles Kelly printed in 1945 showed Ireland as a *spéirbhean* shaking hands with the Taoiseach. It was the time of his measured response to another of Churchill's hysterical outbursts, made immediately after the war in Europe, about the Irish 'frolicking with the

Germans' but there was also the implication that part of the gratitude was for keeping her out of the war.

The other 'enemy' of Ireland was David Gray, the American Ambassador in Dublin from 1940 until 1947. Married to an aunt of Eleanor Roosevelt (1884–1962), FDR's talented wife, he was seventy when he was first appointed and with his patrician Yankee background he had no empathy with Irish-America and avoided contact with them except when painfully necessary. Strictly speaking, Éire was not entitled to a full ambassador; Gray's official title was 'Envoy Extraordinary and Minister Plenipotentiary'. Unlike Maffey, he made no effort to get on terms with de Valera or others members of the government and it was probably because of his reports to FDR that Frank Aiken (1898–83), the Minister for Defence, was received so coldly by the president when he went seeking arms and ships for Éire's defence. Their meeting on 7 April 1941 became acrimonious when FDR said that what Éire had to fear was German aggression. Aiken countered with 'Or British aggression,' and FDR responded angrily with, 'I've never heard anything so preposterous in all my life.' Then in an uncharacteristic burst of temper he ripped the cloth from the table, scattering the cutlery. (This encounter was different from the way that de Valera had been treated by Woodrow Wilson (1856–1924) only in temperature; he was met with glacial politeness but achieved as little.) The American practice of offering diplomatic posts as political or social rewards sometimes meant that very undiplomatic people were appointed to fill them. Even FDR had little time for the 'hyphenated' Irish-Americans, though he needed them in 1932 and in subsequent elections to get elected. Gray was astute enough, however, to take the measure of de Valera describing him in November 1940 to FDR as:

> ...probably the most adroit politician in Europe and he honestly believes that all he does is for the good of the country. He has the qualities of martyr, fanatic, and Machiavelli. No one can outwit him, frighten him or brandish [sic] him. Remember he is not pro-German nor personally anti-British but only pro-de Valera. My view is that he will do business on his own terms or overcome by force.

Gray was sufficiently obtuse to believe that in the weeks before D-day (6 June 1944) when the Allies were to make their main thrust into Europe, German spies, with whom he believed Éire was riddled, would leak the plans to the Axis forces using the wireless equipment set up in the offices of the German representative, Dr Eduard Hempel (1887–1972) in 58 Northumberland Road, not realising that Dan Bryan and his men of G2 had long ago swept the place of all equipment, even an ordinary radio receiver.

Relations with Gray remained uneasy. He was not the most sympathetic choice but he was a man whom FDR accepted at his word since their views of the neutral island were similar. This was to become obvious and rancorous at the time of the so-called 'American Note', written on 21 February 1944, as mediated through Gray but coming as an instruction from the United States government. It included such carefully worded but intrinsically offensive and factually untrue sentences as:

Despite the declared desire of the Irish government that its neutrality should not operate in favour of either of the belligerents, it has in fact operated and continues to operate in favour of the Axis powers…Axis agents enjoy almost unrestricted opportunity for bringing military information of vital importance from Great Britain and Northern Ireland and from there transmitting it by various routes and methods to Germany…We request therefore that the Irish government take appropriate steps for the recall of German and Japanese representatives in Ireland…We should be lacking candour if we did not state our hope that this action will take the form of severance of all diplomatic relations between Ireland and these two countries. You will, of course, readily understand the compelling reasons why we ask, as an absolute minimum, the removal of these Axis representatives, whose presence in Ireland must inevitably be regarded as constituting a danger to the lives of American soldiers and to the success of Allied military operations.

The hidden agenda now seems clear; Gray simply wanted to discredit de Valera and hoped to undo his carefully preserved neutrality. This was not diplomacy but personal animus. It must have given the Axis forces a propaganda victory to seem to have persuaded Gray that they had the capacity to relay this information, in the unlikely event that they could acquire it.

De Valera took no immediate action, risking the anger

of the 'hyphenated' Irish-Americans who were firmly behind their government and whose sons and daughters were in the various branches of the armed forces. The ostensible reason for the Note was the approach of the Second Front and the huge number of US forces in Northern Ireland preparing for it. Grey could not have known just how secure G2 had made all systems of communications. What he suspected was probably true: that de Valera's personal relations with Maffey and Hempel were cordial to the point of friendship. (After the war Maffey was able to say of his relations with de Valera: 'We were both able to look each other in the eye and to believe what the other said.') De Valera's response to the Note came that same day:

> As long as I am here, Éire will not grant this request; we have done everything to prevent Axis espionage, going beyond what we might really be expected to do, and I am satisfied that there are no leaks from this country…the German Minister, I am satisfied, has behaved very correctly and decently and as a neutral we will not send him away.

Robert Brennan (1881–1965), the Irish representative in Washington (1938–47), called without an appointment to the State Department insisting that the Note was an ultimatum. He was reassured that it was merely 'strong advisory' but de Valera sensed that his formal neutral stance was once again incomprehensible to the United States, having been so for nearly five years to the British. More even than at the time of the bombings, he felt that Éire was in some danger. Again the prospect of some occupation by foreign troops – this time of the US – loomed large. He immediately sent for Aiken and had him put Irish forces on full alert, especially along the border. He chose Cavan, one of the border counties, to make a speech warning of a possible danger:

> It is a time of extreme danger…No words which I can use would be strong enough to express my conviction of the necessity of maintaining forces at their maximum strength and efficiency.

That danger, like other threats, passed and the war ended with Éire still neutral but not necessarily proud. There were several occasions when invasions either by Germany or by Britain seemed possible. To magnify the danger is probably wrong especially after Operation Sealion was delayed by the success of the Battle of Britain and the tactically disastrous decision by Hitler to drive east against Russia. Fortress Europe still held firm and the Führer showed a strange reluctance to make absolute enemies of Britain, perhaps hoping to reach some kind of agreed alliance that would enable him to march against America without the destruction of the British Empire, which he was said to admire.

The shocking but not untypical action of de Valera in going to 58 Northumberland Road to offer diplomatic condolences on the news of Hitler's suicide has continued to cause much argument for and against. Some have seen it as a tribute to his cordial relations with Hempel; others see it as evidence of de Valera's utter rigidity in matters of protocol. (There is also the possibility that he did it to assert his ultimate independence and that of his country.) The Jewish community in Ireland, mainly in Dublin and Cork, were thunderstruck, and even supporters of de Valera noted that no other representative of a neutral state had visited German embassies. Maffey called it 'an unwise step'. De Valera suggested that he was expressing his condolences to the German people through Hempel, who had not himself been a member of the Nazi party until compelled to make a purely formal application. Knowing the temper of the man he was neither surprised nor very disturbed by the universal condemnation of his action in America, relayed almost gleefully by Gray. De Valera had not much to do with Harry S. Truman (1884–1972), the unknown vice-president, who had replaced FDR on the latter's death of a cerebral haemorrhage on 12 April 1945. *He* had such things as the atomic bombing of Nagasaki and Hiroshima on his mind and the looming problem of Stalin's Russia. De Valera did try to persuade James Francis Byrnes (1879–1972), the US Secretary of State, to call Gray home but he did not achieve his request until June 1947. There were no tears on either side at his parting.

Even de Valera must have wavered a little because of the reaction to his visit. He found it necessary to reply to Brennan's report on American reaction:

> I have noted that my call on the German minister on the announcement of Hitler's death was played up to the utmost. I expected this. I could have had a diplomatic illness but, as you know, I would scorn that sort of thing…So long as we retained our diplomatic relations with Germany, to have failed to call upon the German representative would have been an act of unpardonable discourtesy to the German nation and to Dr Hempel himself.

During the whole of the war, Dr Hempel's conduct was irreproachable. He was always friendly and invariably correct – in marked contrast with Gray. I certainly was not going to add to his humiliation in the hour of defeat.

Hempel had lived in Dún Laoghaire since 1937 but with the fall of Hitler and the Third Reich there was no salary coming to support him or his wife, Eva. She, like the good *Hausfrau* she was trained to be, supported the family by baking cakes for sale, which the Dublin wits inevitably dubbed 'Hun buns'.

Even a man so noted for his sangfroid as de Valera must have breathed more freely when the war in Europe ended on VE-day, 8 May 1945. Only then was it revealed how complete German plans for invasion were after Dunkirk and the fall of France in the summer of 1940. *Fall Grün* (Operation Green) involved plans, for example, for the landing of 4000 troops on the south coast between Waterford and Dungarvan. These were aborted about the time of Sealion. Historical speculation is always a vain occupation but with such a presence of trained German soldiers on Irish soil it is hard to see what de Valera could have done and what meaning neutrality might have had that summer. It did not happen and the cocooning of Ireland continued. The state of emergency was not lifted until 31 August 1946. In a speech to the nation on Raidió Éireann on 16 May 1945 de Valera rightly praised, among others, '…all those who at heavy personal sacrifice, joined the army, including the Marine Service, and the various auxiliary defence organisations and helped to guard us against the most serious of all the dangers that threatened.' It was well, however, that these groups were never actually put to the test.

## 2

## BUILDING UP DEFENCES

As the use of bombers in Eritrea, Abyssinia and Spain had made clear, the waging of war had fundamentally changed since the trenches of Flanders. Because of aerial bombing, civilians were now in the front line of modern war and preparations had to be made to help them survive. The Government Publications Sales Office in College Street, Dublin, offered a number of Air Raid Precautions (ARP) handbooks. (Originally in Éire ARP stood for Air Raid Protection but this proved to be too ambitious and too optimistic so the British version became used here too.) The cheapest cost one penny and was called *Protection of Your Home against Air Raids*. By comparison *Duties of Air Raid Wardens* cost twopence and *Air Raid Precautions for Animals* set animal lovers back fourpence.

There is inevitably an air of unreality about these booklets, with their insistence on the need for first-aid kits, windowpanes strengthened by tape, buckets of sand and water and determining the safest place in the house during bombardment – usually under the stairs. Unlike Northern Ireland there were no blackout regulations and no assumed need for air-raid shelters. Éire took it that her greatest security was the recognition by Germany of her neutrality and the Reich's ultimate respect for it. The ordinary people chose not to consider how vulnerable they might be and one of the greatest pleasures that the many British and other visitors experienced during the war was the sight of Dublin lit up like a birthday cake.

In Belfast and Derry attitudes were not dissimilar. The people accepted the blackout and the presence of soldiers and sailors, the latter contributing to a much greater social life in the moribund second city. All stayed calm, secure in the knowledge that Ireland as a whole was out of range of the *Luftwaffe*, the heavy bombers needing to conserve enough petrol to return safely to base. Derry was, however, by any logistical calculation a very appropriate target for the German air force, especially since it was an active naval base, with a busy refitting dry-dock, a submarine servicing port and the site of an anti-U-Boat training school. Even before America's entrance into the conflict at the end of 1941, it was likely at any time to have been full of destroyers and corvettes (including American vessels negotiated by Churchill from FDR under the 'lease-lend' arrangement). As the shirt capital of Europe its factories made uniforms for the forces and in its favour in the matter of security it was less than three miles, at its nearest point, from neutral County Donegal – in all a plum catch for visiting Junkers.

Belfast, seventy air miles to the east and that much nearer to Europe was an even more obvious target with the stream of cruisers, destroyers, corvettes and even two aircraft carriers pouring out of its famous shipyards. Belfast shipyards were responsible for a total of nearly 400 of these lighter battleships. Its aircraft factories turned out 133 Sunderland flying boats and 238 Stirling bombers; works in Carrickfergus, twelve miles away, made components for 550 tanks. The famous Belfast rope works supplied cable, rope and cords for all three services. The city's glory days as Linenopolis were briefly revived to make parachutes, sails and other wartime fabric products, and Gallaher Ltd provided the millions of Park Drive cigarettes that were the only rival of Woodbines with the forces.

The *Luftwaffe* could just about reach Liverpool on the Mersey but Belfast on the Lagan, a further 120 miles to the north-west, would have caused some strain. All this changed by the end of June 1940. Germany controlled France, Belgium, Holland, Denmark and Norway; Belfast and Derry were no longer 'out of range'. And, although no one actually said so, Dublin and Cork were within range also. In the circumstances, neutrality seemed the best defence but national pride and pragmatism demanded that the defence forces be put on high readiness and their numbers increased. It was also decided that specific attention should be paid to the possibility of air raids. The chance of invasion either by British or German forces may have been slight but it could not be totally disregarded. If an invasion by either side were actually launched, air power, with its capacity for sudden and devastating destruction, combining high explosive and incendiary bombs, would play a significant part in softening resistance behind the 'lines' and demoralising civilians.

Éire had nothing like the natural resources of Britain and was still shaken by the Economic War. Her geographical position required that she depend on merchant shipping for petrol and oil, coal, wheat and other essentials not available nationally. The quasi-nationalised Irish Shipping Ltd (ISL), established by the government in March 1941, helped maintain essential supplies of food and raw materials. British shipping also delivered raw materials and goods in the normal way of trade. Churchill had imposed a kind of trade boycott in 1940 to try to make de Valera think again about the Treaty ports but it had to be abandoned when British trade began to suffer. During the war ISL carried more than 700,000 tons of wheat, 178,000 tons of coal, 63,000 tons of phosphates (necessary as fertiliser), 24,000 tons of tobacco (horrifying by the standards of today's nanny state), 19,000 tons of newsprint and 10,000 tons of timber. The ships were all clearly marked as neutral but in some inexplicable cases this made no difference to the weary or trigger-happy *Luftwaffe* pilots and enthusiastic U-Boat commanders.

The *Clonlara* (22 August 1941), the *Irish Pine* (15 November 1941) and the *Kyle Clare* (23 February 1943) were all torpedoed by U-boats while the trawler *Leukos* was attacked by gunfire from a U-boat which had surfaced near Tory Island. Some other vessels were victims of magnetic mines – a kind of marine collateral damage: the *Ardmore*, a cattle ship (11 November 1940), struck a mine off the Saltees; the *Innisfallen* (21 December 1940), a passenger ship from Liverpool to Dublin, was sunk by a mine but most of the crew and all the passengers were rescued. Those attacked by German aircraft included the *City of Limerick* (15 July 1940), bombed and machine-gunned in the Bay of Biscay; the *Isolda* (19 December 1940), a vessel belonging to Irish Lights, also clearly marked, attacked on the third run by a German bomber; and a collier, the *Kerry Head* (22 October 1940), sunk after an aerial attack off Cape Clear. The *St Fintan* (22 March 1941), a collier en route to Liverpool from Drogheda, was attacked by two German bombers and perished with all its crew. The story of the *City of Waterford* (19 September 1941), rammed by a Dutch trawler, had a kind of typical wartime irony. The crew were picked up by the *Deptford* and transferred to the *Walmer Castle*. This rescue ship was then attacked by a German plane that scored a direct hit on the engine room and she sank with heavy loss of life, including those saved from the *City of Waterford*. The fate of the *Cymric*, bringing coal from Ardrossan to Lisbon remains a mystery. She was last sighted off County Dublin on 24 February 1941 but was not seen again.

Compared with the 2753 merchant ships lost by Britain during the war the Irish losses may seem trivial but since Éire was clearly neutral in theory (and good practice) there should have been no losses at all. Éire listeners, especially in the more densely populated east-coast counties of Wexford, Wicklow, Dublin, Meath and Louth, could receive BBC radio news broadcasts. By this means they were kept well informed of the generally bad news (from Britain's point of view) until the tide began to turn, spurred by America's entrance to the war in December 1941 and the success of the desert campaign at El Alamein in 1943. They were probably aware of the strict censorship of news at home and only the most innocent would have believed that the output of the BBC was not equally slanted. To call Dunkirk 'the retreat that was a victory' was anticipatory Orwellian 'doublespeak'.

Both Raidió Éireann and the BBC were listened to with an attention and discrimination unknown before or since. There was a fairly large minority who hailed every British defeat with relish. It was, after all, only twenty years since the deliberate violence wreaked in Ireland by the Black and Tans and the even more loathed Auxiliaries. The strange, unnaturally accented voice of William Joyce (1906–46), dubbed 'Lord Haw-Haw' by the English journalist Jonah Barrington was listened to with a mixture of glee and trepidation, since his topographical details were unusually precise. His news in English introduced by 'Germany calling! Germany calling! This is the *Reichssender Hamburg*,' was intended as a threat to enemies and a medium for praise of the *Wehrmacht*'s apparently unstoppable victories. The broadcasts *natürlich* gave rise to urban legends. It was generally believed that Haw-Haw had mentioned the 'golden teapot', a well-known icon in Derry's largest grocery store, and had said that the Albert clock in Belfast was due for aerial demolition. Yet the stories were always at third or fourth hand; no one could be found who had actually heard the broadcasts. It was a typical case of '*Dúirt bean liom go ndúirt bean léi*' heightened by wartime hysteria.

It is customary for most commentators to talk of the 'cocooning' of Éire during the emergency years. In fact the blighting breath of war was never far away. As well as the nearly 50,000 Éire citizens who served in the British forces (and 44,000 from the North) some 120,000 people from the south were working in Britain and Northern Ireland. Some who were already employed in Britain had come back home at the outbreak of the war but had soon returned during the 'phoney war'. The war on the Home Front ceased to be phoney by June 1940. Germany controlled Europe from the Arctic to the Pyrenees and although the success of the Battle of Britain blunted the sharp edge of plans for the invasion of Britain, the months from September 1940 until May 1941 saw the pounding of Britain in day-and-night *Luftwaffe* raids. It was known as the Blitz, a British media shortening of the German word *Blitzkrieg* ('lightning war'), a strategy that had been used with great success in Holland. The targets were ostensibly tactical but since they were situated in working-class areas there were many civilian casualties and the workers from Éire shared the terror and occasional glory with their British mates.

For those at home the period of greatest danger of an invasion lasted for an approximate year, from June 1940 to June 1941. The cancelling of Operation Sealion, because of the strength of the Royal Navy, Germany's losses in the air in August and September 1940 and Hitler's tactically disastrous decision to attack the USSR in June 1941, lessened the chances of the success of *Fall Grün* but in essence the Emergency, from a military point of view, ended in the autumn of 1941. By then the defence forces were at their greatest possible strength even though it was believed even by the most sanguine that formal resistance to a German invasion could have lasted no more than a fortnight. The plans at different periods in that fateful year for taking the Treaty ports by storm, considered seriously by the Germans, the British, and even the Americans, were put aside, because with knowledge of what happened during the Tan War and its unremitting guerrilla activities, all the interested parties considered the cost both in men and world reputation for attacking a small defenceless country too great. But as an Irish-born general said about the crucial battle of Waterloo a hundred-and-twenty-five years earlier: 'It was a near-run thing.'

The need for a visible defence force led to a drive for the formation of a volunteer part-time militia. A Local Security Force (LSF) was formed in June 1940, not long after the fall of France had raised the drawbridge and dropped the portcullis on Fortress Europe. It was first seen as an ancillary Garda force mobilised in seven units, one of them armed, for each Garda district. The duties of the unarmed sections were essentially civilian, including traffic control, communications, first aid and ARP. (The full implication of the last of these seemed extremely unlikely but the authorities had to have some support system, however rudimentary, in case the unthinkable should occur.) The LSF were also to be used for night patrols, prepared to challenge paratroopers and deal with unusual events like unaccounted-for lights and, on the coast, unidentified shipping. It was not made clear what they were to do with any paratroopers should they come across them since even members of the armed section were virtually unarmed. The same armed section was required to protect Garda stations and vital installations, and mount armed patrols, especially in Leinster, where the greater part of the population lived, though the environs of Cork, Limerick and Galway were also patrolled.

By September 1940, 180,000 men had joined the LSF, a majority opting for the armed units constituting LSF, Group A. By the New Year it seemed logical to use them for army duty and from 1 January 1941, they were assigned to military control. These armed volunteers were formed into rifle battalions, intended to be used for garrison duties and local defences, and eventually armed with 0.303 Lee Enfields, thus freeing the army in the event of actual hostilities. They were given a new specific title, Local Defence Force (LDF), and retained that name until 1947 when they were reconstituted as *An Fórsa Cosanta Áitiúil* (FCA), still a significant part of Irish life. (The comparison with Britain's Home Guard, the 'Dad's Army' of the famous television comedy programme, is not exact. The LDF could call upon much younger, fitter men, though in the year of formation they were no better equipped that the British force. The Home Guard had been called the Local Defence Volunteers (LDV) when they were first mobilised in May 1940 but one of Churchill's earliest acts when he became prime minister was to give it its homelier, more dramatic name.) The LDF was armed at the beginning from a motley store of shotguns and other sporting pieces, many privately owned, but later they were given 0.300 Springfields for which ammunition was often scarce.

Because of the powers assumed by the government it could organise any means of defence that seemed advisable but the country was poor, there were few natural resources and inevitably there were clashes and some inter-departmental acrimony. The Department of Finance had the ultimate decision in allocation of resources and its priorities were not necessarily those of defence. For the first nine months of the war it was possible to believe that invasion by either side was unlikely. Neutrality would be respected by both Britain and Germany; essentially Ireland was regarded as hardly even a pawn in the global chess game. After Dunkirk, logistics demanded that for the completion of the Reich's ambition Britain must be brought under German rule. Hitler, at first, tried to make a favourable treaty with Churchill but when this was rejected his only option was *Fall Seelöwe* (Operation Sealion). Éire would have provided a convenient back door for west-coast landings in the United Kingdom. At the bleakest time, the early summer of 1940, it seemed that invasion from the north by the British army or from the south by the *Wehrmacht* in a kind of ghastly sprint to see who could arrive first was not only possible but imminent.

The sense of urgency was increased by an intensive campaign of LDF recruitment, especially for the Cyclist Squadrons who were the main mobile force for guard duties and national protection. They, as ever unsafe from Irish humorists, wet and dry, were soon known as the 'Piddling Panzers'. At times the intensity and extent of the recruiting campaign gave rise to occasional unconscious humour. The Great Northern Railway (GNR) terminus in Dublin (now Connolly Station), well known to the northerners who could afford the trip in their search for unrationed meat and drink, was then called simply Amiens' Street. The LDF propaganda posters all carried the admonition: 'You hold the future of the country in your hands!' It was a fine stirring slogan but placed above the male urinal in the station it caused a certain amount of ribaldry.

Ireland's only natural resource was peat. It was not long until all petrol was at first severely rationed and then became virtually unobtainable by civilians except for those in a few reserved occupations, notably clergy and doctors. There were, too, very limited supplies of coal. Attempts were made to adapt boilers and engines for use of 'turf' and to this end bogs were made to play their part in the 'war effort'. Gigantic turf stacks loomed out of the misty drizzle in Phoenix Park and the Dublin–Derry train took six weary hours, the fireman unable to load coal until the train crossed the border at Goraghwood. In Dublin domestic gas was rationed by the simple process of cutting off the supply during peak periods, when housewives would need it for cooking. These peak periods grew longer and longer and the adaptable Dubliners learned to breakfast before 8 am and use that full power period for cooking dinners that would be reheated after power was available in the late evening. For safety reasons because of the possibility of explosions with full gas rushing again through empty pipes a little gas was present in the system even during the off-period. Lit, this tiny flame enabled the population to boil a kettle for tea in less than two hours and an even shorter time was needed to heat enough water for a man to shave or have a boiled egg for a late breakfast. This illicit practice of using the 'glimmer', as the uncomplaining Dubliners called it, brought out the best in local governmental officialdom. The Dublin Gas Company appointed inspectors with right of access to Dublin kitchens with authority to feel if kettles, pans and teapots had any illegal residual heat. It did not take long for the Dublin wits to dub these inspectors in peaked caps 'Glimmer Men'.

Another classical Irish archetype had been created and inevitably he figured in the wartime Christmas pantomimes. One Christmas, the Theatre Royal, Dublin's leading variety house, presented *Mother Goose*, with the extremely tall and thin Noel Purcell (1900–85) in the name part. In one of the comedy scenes Purcell with some 'helpers' was busy preparing a goose for the Christmas dinner. In the middle of the slapstick that required a lot of flour being tossed about, water directed at the front stalls and unmentionable things being done to the stage goose, a doorbell rang. 'Who is there, if you please?' called out the dame in his best Rathgar accent. 'I'm the Glimmer Man,' said the off-stage voice. 'Well, I'm a glamour gel.' – this in more of a Moore Street register – 'Come in and we'll have a bit of gas!'

That was in late 1944 when fears of invasion had long been stilled and the baptism of aerial bombardment merely a painful memory. However, the near-hardship persisted, as ever afflicting the most vulnerable. The swish of car tyres was seldom heard on Dublin thoroughfares although the streets at rush hours, morning and evening, were thronged with bicycles up to six abreast in the otherwise traffic-free streets, except for ambling buses and rattling tramcars. Some with what the envious called a roughness of money adapted their cars to run short distances on gas stored in frames on top. They looked as if smaller barrage balloons, of the kind seen on cinemas newsreels as the main defences against German bombers, had crash-landed on top of the Ford Eights and Standard Tens. Others, even more resourceful, had adapted their cars to be wood-burning chariots and the newsreel cameras made much of the drivers loading up the boiler with wood blocks.

In the north, with the coming of Canadian and American sailors, those in the know managed to secure supplies of the untipped Sweet Caporal, Lucky Strikes, Philip Morris and Camel cigarettes, marked 'for forces use only' and with a tar rating that would have made a present-day medic blench. The most active commerce took place on the black market, especially busy in the border states of Donegal, Cavan, Monaghan and Louth, with the contiguous Northern Ireland counties of Derry, Tyrone, Fermanagh, Armagh and Down happily taking part. These exotic tobaccos were caviare for smokers. Most of them, weary of the perennial signs at outlets saying, 'Sorry, no smokes,' would have accepted even the dreaded Pasha, a Turkish brand with none of the Virginia tobacco that they were used to, instead of the dire and probably lethal vegetable substitutes.

The horse came again into its glory and the clip-clop of hooves and readily available fertiliser once more became characteristic of Irish cities. Even the trusty bicycles, as newspapers called them, using a Homeric epithet that was not always applicable, were vulnerable. Inner bicycles tubes, often available on a quota system in the north, became favourite contraband goods. Safety blades were sharpened on the insides of tumblers and grandfathers 'cut-throat' razors, grown rusty with non-use, were resurrected 'for the duration', to use a buzz-phrase of the period.

Although they had reasonable supplies of petrol, brought from America and the Middle East and protected by British corvettes, the defence forces were not very mobile. Ireland's road system was quite primitive. Main routes between larger towns were tolerable but the many jokes about side-roads and boreens tended to exaggerate very little. The country still had a comprehensive railway network, a legacy of nineteenth-century prosperity and investment, and even where routes had been discontinued the permanent ways were still viable. By this means the Derry–Buncrana line, which had been displaced by buses, was capable of being recommissioned and continued to serve until the autumn of 1949. The distance was about fourteen miles but fired by turf and thoroughly inspected by customs officials at Bridgend on the Donegal border – it was one of the great smuggling routes – the train took an hour to reach Derry. The many summer-evening cyclists who thronged the roads were disappointed if they could not beat the 'Swilly train' into town.

Under these conditions even the most sanguine of defenders could hold out little hope of resistance to an invasion by either of the great powers. The government's critics, and there were many in spite of the trumpeted solidarity in the matter of neutrality and readiness to resist invasion, suggested that the preparations seemed tactically out of date. Even Fianna Fáil supporters complained that Aiken's ideas of defence were set in a period when the two modern weapons of war, the tank and the plane, were still primitive. Now they were the vital elements of Blitzkrieg, saturation bombing followed by rapid transit across any given terrain by the armoured caterpillars. The lack of air power left the country especially vulnerable, even in the extreme case, as one theory went, of delaying one set of invasion forces long enough for the other to come to the rescue.

Even when the immediate threat of invasion passed, the vulnerability of Éire to air attack remained; it had virtually no workable fighter planes to attempt to do what the RAF Hurricanes and Spitfires had accomplished during the Battle of Britain. There was a dearth of anti-aircraft gunnery, no means of making smokescreens, no barrage balloons or searchlights. The arrangements for civilian protection during possible air raids were almost nil. ack-ack (as anti aircraft devices were called using an older alphabetic code for AA) was only part of any defensive plan.

Scarcity of money played its part, as did a mindset among some of the authorities that, having seen threats of invasion prove chimerical, they could be confident also of escaping attack from the air. As it turned out they were almost right but Éire did in the end suffer its own taste of modern war. One of the earliest battles with the Department of Finance was won by the Department of Defence over the matter of coastal look-out posts (LOPs). In this as in the provision of ack-acks, there was considerable criticism of Sean MacEntee. His care of the country's exchequer was admirable, if seeming occasionally parsimonious. Like many of his countrymen he seemed not to take the question of invasion seriously – nor even the general threat of air raids.

The LOPs had the blessing of G2 as a vital part of intelligence-gathering, especially during the Battle of the Atlantic. The skeletons of these primitive structures may still be seen on headlands from Ballagan Head in County Louth clockwise round to Inishowen Head at the mouth of Lough Foyle. The Foileye LOP on the south side of Dingle in County Kerry, was the last to be built, making eighty-three in all. Many of the sites chosen had been watchtowers during the Napoleonic Wars and by the time of full service none was less than four miles from its two neighbours. They were manned by local volunteers of the Marine and Coast Watching Service (M&CWS), who were paid at the rate of serving soldiers, two shillings a day for a 4th-Class private, two shillings and sixpence for a 1st-Class private and four shillings for a corporal. They were also given three shillings a day for meals because they were fed at home and were no burden to army catering. They worked eight-hour shifts but local arrangements permitted twelve-hour duties to allow the volunteers who were farmers time to work their land. There were twelve duties imposed upon coast watchers, perhaps unnecessarily specific and repetitive, but during their initial training in Dublin they became a dodecalogue of biblical gravity:

1. To be always alert, watchful and quick to report
2. To ensure that messages and reports convey a true and accurate picture of matter reported upon
3. Never to relax vigilance during tour of watch
4. To remain at their post until relieved
5. To ensure that message and reports are definite, simple

and brief

6. To ensure they know the location of nearest telephone
7. To understand his mission, what to report, how to report and to whom to report
8. To avoid giving information on his duties or information on the CWS to unauthorised persons particularly as to the location of the report centre for his LOP
9. To report accurately in post log books all events, messages and incidents that occur during tour of watch
10. To establish the identity of all official visitors to the post before disclosing information or allowing inspection of post
11. To prevent unauthorised persons from loitering in the vicinity of LOP
12. To have no unnecessary exposure of light during night watches

The embarrassment implied in No 6 was eventually obviated by equipping the LOPs with telephones, but not before the usual bureaucratic wrangles with the ever-careful Department of Finance.

The LOPs were built to a pattern and surely not for comfort: they were thirteen feet long and nine feet wide. At the business end there were six windows, two set straight facing the sea with two each to left and right at angles of 120°. There was a small fireplace intended for coal which was often not suited to the local supply of turf. Because of their position on sea cliffs LOPs were difficult of access and quite some distance from the nearest telephone. Basic equipment consisted of telescope, binoculars, silhouettes of ships and planes (especially those belonging to the home Air Corps), log book, signal flags and bicycle. The last of these was essential especially in the early months before the LOPs were fitted out with telephones.

The purpose of the LOPs was the surveillance of their sector of the off-shore waters and airspace. At times, in place of a working compass, a plate indicating true north was fixed at the front lookout window. This also gave bearings and distances from local landmarks. As an afterthought, bad weather gear in the form of oilskins was provided. Conditions of service varied: those facing the west and north had to withstand the full fury of south-western gales and the high Atlantic swells associated with their aftermath. To compensate, those facing east and south-east were likelier to be busier since the *Luftwaffe* always flew over the south Irish Sea on their way to targets in Wales, the Mersey towns, especially Liverpool, and the Clyde Valley. During the British Blitz there were few nights when air activity was not reported especially by LOPS 12, 13, 14, 15, 16, which were clustered round Carnsore Point, the south-eastern tip of the country, well known for its recurring mention in meteorological reports.

The efficiency of the LOPs was greatly increased by co-operation with the Air Corps, the main duty of which was coastal patrol. The corps had begun as the School of Aeronautics in 1926 and was taken to be a constituent part of the army. The planes they had were used for navigation training, aerial photography and liaison flights. By the outbreak of the Second World War there were few planes and they were virtually obsolete. They included some Lysanders,

Gloucester Gladiators, Hawker Hinds, Avro Cadets, Avro Ansons, Vickers Vespas and Walrus Amphibians. These were a motley collection of British-made aircraft, none state-of-the-art and not intended as fighters but adequate for patrolling the coastal waters as part of Air Defence Command (ADC).

The Lysander was a two-seater, high-wing monoplane used mainly by the RAF for transport duties and superseded in 1941 by the American P-40 Tomahawks. Their continued use in Britain was in air-sea rescue. The Gloucester Gladiator, a biplane single-seat fighter, was virtually obsolete in Britain in 1937 but proved effective in the defence of Malta. It had four machine guns. The Hawker Hind was a biplane, like the Lysander intended as an army transport plane. The Vickers Vespa was a two-seater biplane of which the Air Corps had at one stage eight, based in Baldonnel, but they were grounded by 1940. The two Avros were light training planes but because of the short life of aircraft during the first two years of the war they were used by British Coastal Command as spotters; ADC used them for the same purpose. The Walrus Amphibians, as the name implies, were seaplanes, with two wings and capable of being lowered by crane from some of the larger ships of the Royal Navy. Like most of the air corps planes they were used in coastal patrols.

Practically all the planes were incapable of 'scrambling' and the few that might conceivably engage enemy aircraft briefly were not capable of rising to the height at which they might encounter them. Three impounded RAF Hawker Hurricanes supplemented the Air Corps strength and did provide the Corps with potential power to shoot down *Luftwaffe* bombers. The 'Hurries' had outnumbered the more famous Spitfires by a ratio of 2:1 in the Battle of Britain and the three based at

Baldonnel were a substantial threat to intrusive aircraft.

The recognition outlines given to the coast watchers were particularly important since all other aircraft would essentially be regarded as hostile. The cooperation of LOPs with the Air Corps can best be seen in their tracking of the Heinkel III that dropped the first German bomb in Ireland. Accurate identification came to be essential as Irish airspace grew ever more crowded especially between the south-east corner and Dublin Bay. Though never up to ideal specifications Éire's ack-ack defences were strategically placed and could conceivably have shot down hostile planes. Their primary purpose, however, was to 'jink' them off their approach flight and prevent their hitting the targets. Several times Irish Air Corps planes were fired at by the defensive gunners on the heavily armed German bombers.

De Valera realised the need for air defence as early as September 1938 during the Sudetenland crisis when it seemed that the Second World War was about to begin: the need, as he put it, 'to put Irish defences into a good state'. He suggested that they needed sixteen 3.7in Vickers Heavy Artillery (HAA) guns, costing £340,000 and forty-four searchlights. These would be required essentially for the defence of central Dublin. An order for sixty-four of the lighter Swedish 40mm Bofors, also seen to be necessary, would have required an extra £300,000. His suggestion caused the Department of Finance to blanch and the Department of Defence to bluster. There was the usual Dáil double-talk about the need to spread the defence budget more widely. With the Munich agreement on 30 September 1938, when Chamberlain's 'piece of paper' brought 'peace in our time', Finance insisted that Defence 'should spread the expenditure over a period of years in order to ease the burden on the exchequer'.

The result was that by the end of the year 1938 the country had four 3in ack-ack guns of pre-Great War vintage and a quarter of the ammunition required to make them effective. When the whole of Czechoslovakia was occupied by the Nazis in March 1939, it was clear that a world war was inevitable. Orders with Britain for an appropriate supply of modern guns were given too late because with the fall of France in June 1940 an embargo was placed on exports of arms. Aiken, as we have seen, was refused arms by America and had not the War Office relented and allowed a limited export of guns, anti-tank rifles and shells, Éire would have been virtually defenceless.

By November 1940 Dublin had a total of fourteen guns and some attempt at anti-aircraft measures, consisting of: two Bofors at what was then called Collinstown airport, an LOP, a sound locator geared to pick up the noise of approaching aircraft and a searchlight on Howth Head, two heavy 3.7in Vickers guns and a searchlight at Clontarf, four of these ack-ack guns and a searchlight at Ringsend, two medium (pre-1914) ack-acks and a searchlight at Booterstown, one searchlight at Dún Laoghaire and a sound locator, searchlight and LOP at Dalkey. Two heavy Vickers HAA guns in Ballyfermot were to protect the west of the city and at Baldonnel Aerodrome in the south-west there were two Bofors. The anti-aircraft placements were logistically sited to defend essential targets like the port and docks, the electrical generating station at the Pigeon House and the oil depot at the North Wall. The coverage was not ideal but represented the best possible allocation of scarce resources. The greatest lack, however, and the most worrying, was of artillery rounds but by the end of 1940 Churchill had removed the embargo on arms export to Éire, having finally realised that they were unlikely to be used against RAF planes and that, in a way, they constituted a real if weak westerly defence.

# 3

## Air Raid Precautions (ARP)

It was logical to argue that should the *Luftwaffe* decide to call, for whatever purpose, its likely targets would be Cork and Dublin (including the extensive conurbation north and south of the capital city) and the larger east-coast towns of Drogheda and Dundalk. The most cogent reason for such air attacks should be as a preliminary to invasion. But this idea remained firmly outside the calculations if not the imaginations of a majority of Éire citizens and indeed of the members of the Fianna Fáil administration and their loyal opposition. The only signal for such a cataclysm would have been the actuality of an invasion of Britain.

Detailed plans for such an invasion, as the Reich's next move after the fall of France, had been in existence for some time. *Fall Seelöwe* in its preliminary stages had been completed with the occupation of the Channel Islands in June 1940. Reichsmarshall Herman Goering (1893–1946), Hitler's deputy, announced the details of *Seelöwe* on 2 August of that year. It consisted of the destruction of Britain's air power and the demoralisation of its people by the saturation bombing of cities and towns through the United Kingdom. This would be followed by an amphibious invasion. It was not beyond the bounds of possibility that an incursion on south-west England and western Wales could originate from the east coast of Ireland. This might have led to an invasion from Northern Ireland by British forces with face-to-face engagement and neutral Ireland as a cockpit.

The success of the RAF (strongly supported by pilots who had escaped from Czechoslovakia, Poland and other occupied European countries) in the Battle of Britain in the late summer of 1940, the stoical refusal of the civilian population to be cowed by the *Luftwaffe* raids over the next nine months, Britain's continuous if tenuous mastery at sea and Hitler's eventual decision to implement *Fall Barbarossa* against Stalin effectively removed the threat of any invasion. What the defence forces could do was prepare for accidental intrusion either by Nazi planes from the continent or through south Armagh by British army patrols foxed as to the exact location of the border (as was everyone except the immediate locals). The contingency plans for the effects of such intrusions were more or less in place by the end of the summer of 1940, the beginning of the period of greatest potential danger that lasted for more than nine months.

The Air Raid Precautions Act (1939) nominated certain east-coast areas for special security measures. Arrangements in Dundalk were replicated by local adjustments in other coastal towns. A control centre was set up under the town hall that had a secure basement with a ceiling three feet thick just under the entrance foyer. Fifteen telephones, then even scarcer than tea, would be manned in case of an emergency and a kind of air-raid shelter prepared under the Market House. Wardens whose ARP training was continuous were supplied with uniform, helmet, gas mask and cape, notebook and pencil (use not specified but understood to be for the grisly recording of fatalities and injured), torch and fire boots. Civilian gas masks were supplied by Dublin: 10,000 for adults, 1500 for children and 900 respiratory chambers for babies. The equipment was without irony the best obtainable for the money available, which was not much. On St Patrick's Day, 1940 partly as reassurance and partly as an exercise in cooperation there was a parade through Dundalk involving the 'Combined Emergency Services'. It was called 'Step Together' and featured members of the LSF, the Order of Malta (an emergency first-aid service), the Red Cross and a group of Marine volunteers. Fortunately, the efficacy of these measures and the competence of the services were hardly ever put to the test.

It was known from study of the experience in Britain that civilian defence should have three main elements: evacuation of children, air-raid shelters and a welfare system for survivors of bombing. (It was only after the devastating raids in Belfast that the problem of disposal of the bodies of the dead was added to the list.) In spite of stringent censorship it was clear from BBC broadcasts, cinema newsreels and British papers what 'safety' steps should be taken. From the beginning of the Emergency there was a flurry of instructions sent to local authorities calling for a reduction of lighting by 75%. Some assiduous local gardaí insisted on a total blackout even in remote villages and, when Ballina and Sligo went dark, the local yobbos took advantage of the cover to indulge in anti-social behaviour. The public was also asked to avoid panic buying and the hoarding of supplies – always a clear invitation to a hysterical populace to do exactly the opposite. Some better-organised housewives bought black cloth and made curtains to cover their windows; others painted some of the window panes black. A new pamphlet entitled *Protect Your Home against Air Raids,* issued urgently by the Department of Defence, spoke of the advisability of taping the windows, having buckets of water and sand for fire extinguishing and building up a supply of long-lasting emergency rations. Books of instructions with such titles as *ARP Practical Guide – for the Householder and the Air-Raid Warden* were rushed into print and were a snip at seven pence (pre-decimal coinage), €1.40 at today's prices.

The flurry of excitement did not last. Some public-spirited citizens volunteered as wardens but their tasks, it was felt, could very well be covered by the LDF and only very rudimentary ARP training was given. There were no formal plans for evacuation of children. When billets were found in the local countryside for 70,000 Belfast evacuees in June 1940 there was a palpable sense of relief, yet when the buses and trains arrived at the collection points only one tenth of the total had come. These 7000 very soon drifted back home, to the delight of some of their temporary hosts. Again when in August 1940 the invasion of Britain seemed a racing certainty and a second Belfast evacuation was arranged, only 1800 of an expected 5000 children turned up. It was only after the severe raids in the spring of 1941 that self-evacuation became a reality and local welfare officials had the job of tending to many children who had walked to the city's periphery.

Evacuation in Éire was viewed as a possible sequel to actual invasion and because of the experience in Belfast anticipatory preparation was regarded as pointless. The one uniting principle was that the needs of the defence forces in all aspects of its work should be paramount and take precedence over those of the civilian population. Those civilians with cars (about 10,000) and an expected 5000 cyclists would be directed out along the main road to Bray and not allowed to use any other route; 41,000 evacuees would be moved by rail. If the site of the German troops landing were near Cork the city would be quarantined with no access or exit for vehicular traffic. If the city were to be evacuated, the refugees might have to walk up to sixteen miles before reaching a transport marshalling point. In the east, arrangements were made for moving 104,000 people to counties Meath, Westmeath, Longford, Leitrim and Roscommon, and 56,000 to counties Wicklow and Wexford. Preparations for invasion, even if not many believed it would happen, were intended to apply equally in the case of severe aerial bombardment. Air-raid shelters were virtually non-existent outside of the city and even in Dublin there were far two few to support the population. It was even suggested that railway tunnels be used as shelters, perhaps as the Londoners used the underground during the Blitz. The comparison was ludicrous: the tube stations were warm and well lit with plenty of space, if only minimum toilet facilities.

As it turned out, the services of the Éire ARP were required earlier than many, including themselves, expected. At least five separate German bombings occurred between August 1940 and February 1941 before any attack on Belfast. Most of them could have been unintentional and none of the targets seemed to be tactical, though there were many local pundits who claimed to see deliberate intentions and patterns in the apparently random events. LOPs in the south-east had reported a sudden increase in German air activity from May 1940 that became intense by the end of the summer to coincide with the beginning of the saturation bombings of British population centres. With the fall of France, Belgium and Holland, airfields much closer to Britain and Éire had become available. For the Dorniers and Heinkels using Evreux and Dreux, north-west of Paris, and Soesterberg in Holland, the flight time to Glasgow, Belfast and Newcastle, once regarded as beyond their fuel capacity, were now within safe reach.

It was, however, something of a surprise that the first bombs to fall on the island of Ireland hit villages in the south of County Wexford on Tuesday, 26 August 1940. Two Heinkel HE-III bombers had been observed coming in low from the Irish Sea over Carnsore Point at 1340 hours. The LOP there identified them merely as two low-winged monoplanes flying at 10,000 feet heading north-west. (By then the LOP observers had become accustomed to overflights; between 20 and 31 August, forty intrusive aircraft were noted.) Greenore LOP, about five miles north-north-east of Carnsore, confirmed the presence of the two bombers and suggested that they were indeed He-IIIs.

The two planes, one about fifty feet above the other, continued along the line of the Rosslare–Wexford railway track and by 1352 they were above Campile, a village near Dunbrody Abbey, about twenty-five miles west-north-west of Carnsore Point, the chief building of which was the Shelbourne co-operative creamery. Here the planes separated, one circling the village while the other turned right about and flew back south-east to drop four 1000-pound bombs when it was over Duncormick, five miles north-west of Kilmore Quay, and the nearby Ambrosetown, fortunately without causing loss of life. One of the bombs damaged the home of

Jim Hawkins, the stationmaster, of Kilmore Quay and the Ambrosetown bombs narrowly missed a railway viaduct.

The first HE-III continued to circle the creamery and came in low enough, at less than four hundred feet, to be observed clearly by locals who saw the black crosses edged with white on the plane's wings and the swastika on the tailplane that identified it as a *Luftwaffe* plane. (The swastika was an old Aryan symbol made of four Greek gammas arranged in a crooked cross, that had been adopted by Hitler's party as early as 1920 and remained a ubiquitous and visible sign of Nazi dominance.) It dived to an altitude of less than two hundred feet to let go a stick of five 500-pound delayed-action high explosives. The first bomb hit the Campile creamery and killed three women who were dining in the canteen: Mary Ellen Kent aged thirty, her sister Catherine Kent aged twenty-six and their friend Kathleen Hurley who was twenty-seven. The toll of fatalities would have been much greater except that the majority of the employees of the creamery had gone home as usual for their midday meal.

The second bomb went through the roof of the grain store, igniting a quantity of fine bran called pollard and starting a fire that was extinguished within five minutes. Clearly the co-op's ARP arrangements were remarkably efficient. The third landed in the creamery yard and disintegrated without exploding while the fourth shattered the canteen window and did some damage to the railway station. The main line was not affected but rails and sleepers in a siding were displaced and twisted. The windows of the stationmaster's house disintegrated and slates flew off the roof. Two young girls received head injuries from glass splinters. The last bomb of the stick fell harmlessly in a field to the north-east but made a crater thirty feet in diameter and fifteen feet deep.

The bombings seemed to the team of investigators to be deliberate; they could not blame poor visibility on a clear sunny day in late August. Visibility was, in fact, exceptionally good up to a hundred miles from the estimated height of the HE-III when the bombs were released. To test the prevailing atmospheric conditions the Air Corps followed the same flight tracks less than one hour later and confirmed that visibility was excellent. The pilots of the bombers had not even the usually offered excuse of defensive fire. Even the tactics of the raid were copybook *Luftwaffe* methods, particularly the *Schleichflug* (literally 'sneak flight') using an almost silent glide approach. For the German authorities to claim, as they often did, that bombings were caused by mistaking the Irish coast for that of England or Wales suggests an incompetence in map-reading that would have disgraced a cub scout.

Such was media wariness about offending the censor and having even greater sanctions imposed that there was minimum coverage of the event. That summer Germany seemed unstoppable and the Department of Foreign Affairs intimated to Hempel that there would be a very low-key response to the story. Raidió Éireann made some muted mention of air intrusion but it was the American papers that had the first full account. The response of Aiken's office to the news was coloured not so much by fear of offending Germany as by its desire to prevent the inevitable outcry from opposite sides of the political spectrum. The anti-German protest would have been much easier to control and face down than the pro-German one, supported inevitably by the IRA. In fact there were no protests since the details were sparse and deliberately unclear.

The reason for an air attack on a co-op in a rural part of Ireland on a summer afternoon was never discovered. If the air crew had merely wished to jettison their load, why not do it safely at sea? Why dive-bomb what was clearly a creamery? Some suggested that the pilot, a little disoriented, believed he was over Wales and thought that the Shelbourne building might just be tactical. It was the day after a heavy night blitz on London that lasted six hours. Germany offered no explanation as to cause. The usual people suggested that the plane was British dropping captured German bombs. An even more ingenious, if extremely unlikely suggestion, was that some British soldiers captured at Dunkirk had sandwiches wrapped in butter paper bearing the name of the co-op and that the creamery was raided in retaliation. Some members of the Defence Forces suggested that it happened because the creamery was known in Germany because of pre-war trade. From 1935 the great number of German tourists in all the Western European countries was later felt to have constituted a kind of low-level observation force sending home information, innocuously written on postcards. Those who supported the theory could point to frequent attacks on the Rosslare–Fishguard mail boat, meant, it was surmised, to discourage cattle exports. The attacks on the railway line and Campile and the station at Ambrosetown might be part of this tactic of attacking 'economic' targets that even remotely 'gave consolation to the enemy', to use the expression current at the time.

Local people later claimed that they knew that the plane was German even before they could see the markings; it was general knowledge that the drone of the engines was intermittent rather than continuous, as with RAF planes.

The German engineers had devised a more fuel-efficient engine, the workings of which generated the characteristic interrupted sound. The locals would not listen to any explanation and made no attempt to exculpate the Nazis. They were very angry at the deaths and the destruction, and when Hempel attended the funeral of the Campile victims wearing a frock coat, tall hat and sash bearing the swastika, security had to be extremely tight with military and civil police forming a safety cordon around him to prevent any attack by the crowd. The final 'not-proven' verdict was that the bombing was a deliberate attack on what was presumed to be a legitimate military target but in the wrong country. The German government made no objection to a local claim for compensation of £18,822/4s/8d, a very precise amount. This was adjusted to £14,500 by the government in Dublin but it accepted the £9000 paid by the German government three years later.

Though there were many overflights in the autumn and winter there were no further serious bombing incidents. Air raids on Britain were reaching a climax in extension and frequency and it was inevitable that the navigators would use the lights of Éire as guidance, aware that the sudden darkening that occurred when they reached the border at Armagh and Down gave them a reassuring pointer as to how far north they were en route to Birmingham and Liverpool. It was a time of great tension in a Britain daily expecting invasion and though expectation in Éire was less sharp the Defence Forces continued on high alert realising that there was little they could do to stop the *Wehrmacht*. Should Germany decide, as was likely, to drop paratroopers on the east coast to establish a springboard to Britain from the west, a few days' delay was all the Irish could hope for. It was strongly felt that the Axis forces would prefer not to invade Ireland if possible but that if they thought it necessary they would not hesitate. Dublin was the appropriate place to set up the (temporary?) alternative government before negotiation and armed might would give them untroubled access. The nearest LOP to the south of the capital was at Dalkey and the sentinels were instructed to 'keep a sharp look out for aircraft, searchlight station to stand by'. The bombers came regularly about midnight, wave after wave, but they tended to go either east or west, bypassing the capital before turning left for Liverpool.

This uneasy peace was disturbed once, on 25 October, when four high explosives and a hundred incendiaries were dropped in open countryside near Rathdrum, County Wicklow, with minimum damage. Then at 1900 hours on Friday, 20 December, bombs and flares were dropped on Dún Laoghaire and Sandycove in County Dublin. The Howth LOP spotted a plane flying south at 1926 hours. 'Blinding flares' were seen and bombs did some damage to Sandycove Station, although a train just then arriving at the platform was undamaged.

The previous day Hempel, through Joseph Walshe, the permanent secretary at the Department of Foreign Affairs, had informed the government that Berlin required their legation to be supplemented by four extra civilian staff and proposed to land them in Ireland as soon as permission was obtained. A civilian airliner, a Junker Ju-52, would deliver them at Rineanna, the western airfield in County Clare, that, having been chosen as an airport in 1936, became operational in 1939 and later formed the nucleus of Shannon airport. The threat of 'Sealion' had abated somewhat perhaps from code 'red' to code 'yellow' but the possibility of the use of Éire as a backdoor to attack Britain from the west remained. It was clear that the four 'civilians' were military attachés and de Valera and Aiken considered that their presence would be seen as an infringement of neutrality. In a way this was the most courageous stand that de Valera and his supporters took throughout the war. Germany, as we have seen, was at the height of its power and resistance to a *Wehrmacht* invasion with paratroopers and dive-bombers would scarcely have lasted a week. Hempel warned the Irish government that refusal of this simple request would be regarded 'in a most serious light'. The diplomatic impasse lasted for about a week.

The Irish government reacted by cancelling all military leave and placing the ARP, fire service and LSF on full alert. When Hempel saw how determined the Irish government was to resist the ukase he spoke urgently to the German Foreign Office and personally to Joachim von Ribbentrop (1893–1946), the German foreign minister, to advise him that from his reading of the situation Irish attitudes would only harden if Germany persisted. In fact there were no immediate plans to invade. Sealion was put on hold and any invasion of Éire on its own would have been logistically meaningless. At the time the extra sea journey of any landing craft even as far as Wexford would have left them vulnerable to the Royal Navy and the fighters of the RAF. De Valera and Aiken did not know this, although Walshe, who could read Hempel very well, may have guessed it.

When a short time later two bombs were reported to have fallen in Shantouagh, near Carrickmacross in County Monaghan, some Irish officials suggested that the bombing was first of all a show of *Luftwaffe* strength and that it was entirely possible that the largely pointless bombing had a punitive element to it. If a simple request to increase embassy staff could excite de Valera and Aiken so much it was likely that some change of tactics would be employed. Most Irish people believed that these mid-winter 'raids' might have been the results of errant planes getting rid of unused bombs. These individual strays could possibly have been part of a strong *Luftwaffe* squadron that had been targeting the Mersey and the important docks in Liverpool and Birkenhead.

Throughout the country there was little awareness of these events thanks to lack of detailed news coverage of yet another 'bombing incident' and no one realised until afterwards that Hitler had suspended raids on Britain on Christmas Day and St Stephen's Day. The Christmas lull in Ireland lasted for about a week. Then on 29 December a JU-88 reconnaissance plane flew in over Tramore, going west of Dublin to Navan where it turned and flew back over the city. Later documents showed that the Junkers photographed Baldonnel aerodrome and the level approaches from it to the city as a possible reconnaissance before a para-landing. It flew away without further incident but the first three days of the New Year saw more intrusions and the first bombs on an Irish city.

Targets on New Year's Day 1941 were Duleek and Julianstown, towns six miles apart in County Meath. Eight bombs fell, causing little damage and no injuries. The next morning just after six o'clock two bombs fell in Rathdown Park, part of a nest of similarly named streets between the Templeogue and Rathfarnham Roads in Terenure in south Dublin, destroying two houses and injuring seven people. One bomb damaged the semi-detached home of Mr and Mrs Edward Plant and that of the Isaacson family who lived close by. They were trapped when the back wall fell in on top of them. The Dublin fire service sent two pumps and alerted two ambulances. By the time they reached the site on a snowy winter morning they found that all but one of the inhabitants who had been trapped by fallen masonry had been removed by the ARP service and were on their way to hospital. The houses of W.T. Murphy, a well-known sports correspondent and that of his neighbour, Simon Lapeden, Nos 46 and 48 Rathfarnham Road, had huge boulders crash through the roofs. Young Stanley Lapeden avoided serious injury when a rock came through the ceiling to land beside his head on the pillow.

Olive and Dorothy Murphy, W.T.'s daughters, extricated themselves from the debris of their home and, with their brother, Tom, rushed to Rathdown Park where the first bomb had fallen. They had some training in First Aid – Olive was an active member of St John's Ambulance Corps – and they were guided to the scene by the cries of distress from the victims. The chief fire officer caused the local streetlights to be switched off because he could still hear the noise of the engines of at least one German plane still circling above. Other bombs landed, one on waste ground in Fortfield Road on the west side of Templeogue Road, and others at Lavarna Grove in nearby Kimmage. No one was hurt but houses were damaged over a large area.

Dublin City Council's archives list claims for compensation from Rathdown Villas, Fergus Road, Lavarna Road, Bushy Park Road and Zion Road. Carrying the story without hesitation unlike its more circumspect reporting of events in Northern Ireland, the *Derry Standard* on Friday 3 January, gave names and places. (Its coverage of the bombing of Derry six weeks earlier had the uninformative headline; 'Raid on a Northern Ireland town.') It noted:

> The Prime Minister, Mr de Valera, was at Government Buildings all day yesterday morning and late in the afternoon receiving reports of the various bombings. He did not leave for lunch until after the official statement for the Press had been prepared. As he walked down the steps of Government Buildings to his car he looked very grave and preoccupied.

He would have greater reason for looking grave by the time the paper was on the streets. The next morning at 3.15 the *Luftwaffe* returned, again inexplicably but with greater force. The centre of attention was the Donore city council area that includes Dolphin's Barn and the South Circular Road, and it was here that what just might pass for tactical targets were damaged. The first point of impact was Donore Terrace but damage was widespread. The second bomb demolished two houses, Nos 91 and 93 South Circular Road and seriously damaged fifty others. In all thirteen people were trapped under rubble but although some of their injuries were serious all survived. One of the attending firemen fainted from gas inhalation from a fractured mains source.

Among the non-domestic buildings hit or damaged by this blast were the Presbyterian Church on Donore Terrace, the Boyne Linen Company and the Hospice for the Dying, both in Harold's Cross. However, the majority of damaged buildings were located on the South Circular Road: the Greenmount and Boyne Linen Company, the White Swan

Laundry, Wills Cigarette factory (makers of the widely popular Woodbine brand, untipped and lethal, and known even then as 'coffin nails'), the National Boxing stadium, St Catherine's Rectory and a synagogue. This last target was considered very significant by those very knowledgeable men who had a much better grasp of national and international affairs than anyone in the government, in spite of never seeming to budge from their hallowed seats in the corner of the snug. They pointed to the name of the owner of the house hit in Rathdown Park, clearly Jewish. (They weren't sure about Lapeden but they had their suspicions.) It was the damage to the synagogue on the South Circular Road that convinced them utterly that they knew the reason for the raid. The Nazis, it seemed, were targeting the Jews worldwide.

These first raids in the capital had a predictable reaction. *The Irish Times* of Saturday 4 January, risking, as was their game, the wrath of the censor, praised the courage of the security services. It was rather dangerous to mention German raids at all but to make them the subject of an editorial calling for even greater dim-outs of city streets and berating P.J. Hernon, the city manager, for not alerting the total population was asking for trouble from the censor. Hernon excused himself on the grounds of proportionate response, ever conscious of the need not to spread alarm and despondency. His view was that using alarm signals in a peaceful country would be inadvisable in that it might frighten 'people over a wide area because of what is perhaps an isolated incident'. Compared with the nightly pounding suffered by British cities the raid was trivial; even Belfast was to suffer much more death and destruction four months later.

The difference that the ARP blackout regulations in Ulster

made to the night sky was most obvious in the border town of Pettigo in South Donegal through which the Northern Ireland border ran, dividing the town in two. On one side of the main street shop windows glowed like Christmas while on the other ARP wardens with partly masked torches patrolled to check that no chink of light should show through the heavy blackout curtains. Pettigo was too far west to be of much interest to the Germans but to the east the contrast between the Stygian County Down and its well-lit neighbour County Louth was striking. Those who argued for full lighting along the border counties were probably right. Light against dark was a good determinant of where hostile Ulster ended and neutral Éire began.

Even after the January raids, once things had become 'normal' again, it was hard to take the *Luftwaffe* threat seriously, especially when government control of the media tamped down the exact nature of that threat. There were other more serious incidents in those first days of January. On the morning of 2 January a stick of eight bombs was released over the townland of Knockroe, near Borris in County Carlow, close to the border with Kilkenny. There were then only about six well-scattered dwellings in Knockroe and the bombs hit the house of a family called Shannon, demolishing it. There were eight people staying there that night: John Shannon, his wife Mary Ellen, son Raymond, daughter Kathleen and his sister Brigid, John's brother Patrick and his sons, James and Michael. All the men survived but the three women were killed instantly. The location was so remote, the house clearly not a tactical target, without any element even of political significance, that no reasonable cause could be discovered.

There had been, of course, no warning and no real

explanation followed. A suggestion by the German authorities that the pilot mistook the east coast of Ireland for the west coast of Wales seems bizarre. With Atlantic weather the norm even in the south-east of the country it might be difficult to distinguish sea from land but to mistake an east coast for a west one suggests some serious misreading of charts. The likeliest explanation was that, as in Derry the following Easter, the pilot decided to offload his bombs for safety when he had to land again in France.

Later that day, at about 7.45, pm a single plane flew over Ballmurn in County Wexford and dropped a line of bombs without causing any injuries but leaving deep craters and one unexploded high explosive bomb. This was afterwards safely dealt with by the defence forces. The fact that many of the bombs were low-grade incendiaries suggested again that the pilot was simply dumping extra ballast. In general, east Leinster was subject, over the early days of January, to bombs, high explosives, incendiaries and, strangely, sea-mines falling apparently at random. Two of these, floating eerily down with their ghostly parachutes, looking like exotic blooms, landed without exploding at Kilcormack, near Enniskerry, just over the border between Dublin and Wicklow. These were defused on the afternoon of Friday, 3 January. Bombs also fell near the Curragh, several on the Aga Khan's 200-acre stud farm. One unexploded high explosive sank itself to a depth of six feet into the ground, causing the house of the Aga's agent to shudder as if as a result of a bomb blast. (None of the pub savants, as far as it is known, suggested that Hitler had it in for Muslims as well.) The Kildare fire brigade was on the scene quickly and put out a fire in the haysheds of James Cox, in Walshestown, near Newbridge.

At first, those who were happy to believe anything accepted the communiqué issued by Karl Heinz Petersen of the German news agency that the British were to blame. James Dillon, who alone in the Dáil disapproved of de Valera's neutral stance, demanded that Aiken make it clear that the *Luftwaffe* were involved. It was soon established that the bombs were of German origin but this information was either withheld or downplayed. No sensible person believed the German government's statement that the bomber pilot had confused the two coasts. It was argued rather forcefully that they didn't know their right hands from their left (or that they confused other parts of their bodies). The wise men in the corners said that their maps were upside down and sure didn't they all drive on the wrong side of the street anyway.

Dublin Corporation immediately set in motion a plan to repair the damages done in Donore and was responsible for implementing the government's compensation arrangement detailed in a bill passed later that year as the Neutrality (Damage to Property) Act. There was deserved praise for the emergency services, both statutory and voluntary.

The majority of people knew that the raids had been carried out by the *Luftwaffe*, although atavistic and instinctive anti-British feeling continued. Although aware that the scattered and spasmodic raids were only to be expected in time of war most people felt that their neutral status was still their best protection and that they had had a baptism of fire that was unlikely to be repeated. Six deaths, although sad for family and friends, could be borne by the population at large.

Restrictions on newspaper coverage prevented emotional exploitation of the events of that January, one of the reasons for Aiken's censorship instructions. The near-ban on detailed reporting did, however, greatly increase rumours.

The German authorities made little attempt to explain the raid, let alone apologise. Though Walshe protested on 3 January, advising Hempel that the incidents were 'causing the greatest perturbation to the government and amongst our people' he got no satisfaction. The German legate covered his undoubted embarrassment with diplomatic bluster, especially when Walshe warned that if such 'carelessness' continued, they 'would be obliged to conclude that they [the raids] were due to a deliberate policy on the part of the German government'. Aiken 'hoped and believed' that the three days of bombings had been 'mistakes due to weather conditions in conjunction with concentrated raids on British west-coast towns'. Hempel at first blamed the British but since he did not believe this version himself it was hard for him to convince anyone else. His aide-de-camp, Henning Thomsen, was rather impatient with the Irish as they asked for explanations. He dismissed their objections with the equivalent of a diplomatic shrug saying that Éire had been 'very lucky in this respect so far' not to have had more bombing attacks. With the more intensive aerial activity over England that would be unavoidable from then on, 'there were bound to be mistakes'. He implied that with the intense focus on the job in hand Luftwaffe pilots and crew might easily stray out of the optimum flight path. With the speed at which their bombers had to fly, a drift of fifty miles could be regarded as negligible. It gave G2 (with whom Thomsen had been talking) and the government little comfort but since both Britain and America refused to supply arms – ack-ack, shells, searchlights and the other defence equipment – there was little they could do except maximise the efficiency of the forces and weaponry it possessed.

# 4

## Solidarity

By the spring of 1941 the emergency services were as ready for action as they could be, the volunteers of the LDF and the Auxiliary Fire Service complementing the various full-time statutory bodies like local fire services and the Irish Red Cross. Their first great test – out of which they emerged with some glory – did not occur in their own jurisdiction but after an early-morning race north to help with fire-fighting during the terrible raid on Belfast on the night of 15/16 April.

It was Easter Tuesday, with many adults and all the school-children still on holiday. Up to two hundred bombers, Heinkels and Dorniers, from bases in Evreux and Dreux north-west of Paris, flew up the middle of the Irish Sea to avoid the radar stations on the Welsh coast and the single County Down emplacement at Kilkeel. They went west of the Mourne Mountains and Slieve Croob, flying over Dromore and up the Lagan basin to reach their targets, the shipyards and industrial centres clustered on both sides of Belfast Lough. The reading of terrain from the bomb-bay of a plane is a special skill and even then experts can be misled by cloud, flight path and other factors. It was believed that the saturation bombing of the ordinary dwellings on the Antrim, Cavehill, and Shankill

Roads was caused by an aerial misinterpretation of the city waterworks with its pallid reflected light for the larger and wider Belfast Lough.

The raid began at 2240 as wave after wave of bombers dropped 200,000 high explosive bombs with special whistles attached to the tailplanes to make them sound more frightening. They fell on sub-standard working-class terraced houses, many at least a hundred years old and in such poor condition that a direct hit on one dwelling was enough, with blast and domino effect, to demolish a whole street. The tradition of workers living close to the mills was paying a negative dividend. The first wave consisted, as usual, of the dropping of parachute flares to illuminate the targets to the sortie. These ghostly vertical will-o'-the-wisps came silently down, dancing a little in the breeze that had scattered the city's cloud cover and revealed a moon, three-quarters full. Then came the parachute mines, timed to go off just above ground to maximise their destructive capacity. The high explosives did frightful damage but the 96,000 firebombs had greater destructive power because of the continuing damage they were able to inflict.

Fires burned all night long, still wreaking damage after the raiders had departed. The last All-Clear was not sounded until 5 am on the Wednesday morning. The whole complement of full-time firefighters and members of the hurriedly trained Auxiliary Fire Service (AFS) were called out and they did what they could to extinguish the infernos, fanned by mild spring breezes. Perhaps here Nazi intelligence was more accurate than was realised. In a previous visitation on the Tuesday of Holy Week, a week earlier, six Heinkels (one of which was later shot down) had killed fifteen people and done considerable damage around the docks. Some of their high explosives had fractured mains and with no water supply the fire services were unable to help much. This has led some historians to suggest that this more recent attack on the waterworks was not in mistake for the shipyards but a deliberate move to render fire-fighting impossible by depriving the service of water.

Like the rest of the country the population of Northern Ireland had firmly believed that they were secure from air raids. This insouciance manifested itself in a woeful lack of civilian security. Air raid shelters were few and not very sheltering; there were no searchlights, no means of laying down protective smokescreens and few barrage balloons. These latter were huge gas-filled blimps just discernible at 7000 feet where they swayed gently as if impaled on their vertical steel cables. Their hoped-for purpose was to prevent bombers flying low for more precision bombing and using their machine guns on any civilians rash enough to stray out of shelters during raids. According to War Office recommendations a city like Belfast should have had twenty-four Bofors 40mm and 3.7-inch heavy ack-ack guns (HAA); in fact they had only two Bofors and seven HAAs. Extra fire-fighting equipment that Scotland had offered as a matter of urgency in 1940 was refused by the Northern Ireland cabinet as superfluous to requirements.

The blinkered attitudes of the Northern Ireland government, giving a greater priority to frugality than security, changed with the appointment of John MacDermott (1896-1979) as Minister of Home Security in 1940. He was a steadfast Unionist, MP for Queen's University and Lord Chief Justice from 1951, but younger and more aware of the realities of the situation than his complacent, elderly cabinet colleagues. He had visited the bombed cities of Britain, especially Coventry, Glasgow and Liverpool, and knew what devastation the *Luftwaffe* was capable of inflicting on urban centres. He did what he could to obtain more ack-acks, searchlights and smokescreen equipment. His crash programme of building brick shelters with reinforcing steel rods saved many lives but they had to be built above ground and so provided no shelter against direct hits. Central Belfast is built on sleech, a wet, peaty, mobile swamp and could not sustain subterranean building without very expensive shoring.

It became obvious by midnight on Easter Tuesday that the existing emergency services were intolerably hard-pressed and would soon be unable to deal with the damage that was being inflicted. It was then that R.D. Harrison, City Commissioner of Police, rang MacDermott with a practical suggestion that was wise but at the same time potentially explosive. He put it to him that help should be sought from the South. It was a difficult call. MacDermott, like all members of the Northern Ireland government, barely recognised de Valera as head of state and utterly rejected his claim as Taoiseach for a return of the six counties severed from the country. He, like his cabinet colleagues, had looked with amused condescension amounting to disrespect on what they still called with a slight sneer, the 'Free State' and its government. Yet he could not ignore the fact that thousands of fires had been started and the waves of bomb-runs were apparently endless. Help was desperately needed. The other near source of aid was Scotland but transport across the North Channel took time to organise while Dublin was just over a hundred miles away on land. He thought the risk worth taking and rang Sir Basil

Brooke (1888–1973), the deputy prime minister, who gave assent, noting in his diary entry that the move was 'obviously a question of expediency'. Brooke remained a hard-line Unionist but misery acquaints us all with strange bedfellows. (MacDermott wisely chose to consult Brooke rather than his chief John Andrews (1871–1956), whom Brooke would soon succeed. Andrews's indecisiveness meant that no action would have been taken before the need had passed.)

MacDermott must have understood that the Unionist position, though problematic, was less fraught than de Valera's. How could the carefully preserved neutrality of Éire be reconciled with aid and support to a belligerent? Northern Ireland was legally part of Britain and succour to the beleaguered city could be interpreted as a warlike attack on Germany. De Valera later exculpated himself with his usual forensic skill, his position later stated by Aiken to American journalists: 'Of course, we should go to Belfast. They are Irish people too.' De Valera himself spoke at a meeting at Castlebar on 19 April a few days after the event: '…they are all our people – we are one and the same people – and their sorrows in the present instance are also our sorrows, and I want to say that any help we can give them in the present time we will give them wholeheartedly, believing that were the circumstances reversed they would also give us their support wholeheartedly.' It was disarming and for once pleased everyone – except the Germans.

The precise sequence of the events of the night is far from clear but there was no doubt about the result. At 6.10 am on the Wednesday morning, Major J.J. Comerford, the Dublin fire chief, recorded that three pumps, two manned by full-time Dublin fire-fighters and a third by the now competent AFS, were approaching Belfast from the south-west. Three other appliances were dispatched from Dundalk, Drogheda and Dún Laoghaire. The shadowy blacked-out southern counties of Armagh and Down in stark contrast to the better-lit Louth was a clear indication that they had crossed the border. Police forces north and south had been alerted to give open roads to the Dubliners; customs officers had also been informed.

At first the tenders' headlights were inadequate properly to light the often twisting roads in south Armagh and Down. It was a cold night for the travellers; the fire engines had no roofs because the rescue ladders were layered over the heads of the men, who sat on their hands to ease the chill. The drivers, strangers to the roads, used the telegraph wires as guides but soon the way was made clear as they saw the smoky red glare to the north-east easily overcome the first touches of the spring dawn.

Such a colourful event, regarded by those under forty as near-folklore, inevitably attracted many myths as all good sagas should. One sworn to be true was that the Dennis fire engines came roaring into Belfast flying an inordinate number of green, white and orange tricolours. The tale originated with both communities, nationalists asserting with a certain forgivable triumphalism that 'our lads' were coming to the rescue of the northern city (they had not had much to be triumphal about before this, the Unionists pleased with the gesture but deploring the need to make political capital out of an air raid.) There was no truth in the story; the Belfast caper was just another dangerous 'shout' for the southern fighters; flags and emblems were the last things on their mind. For one thing it would have been against health and safety regulations, even before the unnatural birth of the nanny state. Health and safety also disproved the charming nugget that the charismatic Alfie Byrne (1882–1956) had travelled on the leading pump to underline solidarity. Byrne, an independent TD since the founding of the state, had served as Lord Mayor of Dublin (1930–9) and was a colourful feature of the city where he was known as the 'shaking hand of Dublin', a synecdoche with no pathological significance: he walked in morning-coat and wing-collar about the streets offering his hand to any passer-by who would accept it. The story rose out of the sense of fitness that he should be part of any Dublin adventure but at most he may have travelled as far as Swords in a staff car to see them off at city limits.

Another story has it that the Free-Staters confined their fire-fighting to the Protestant Shankill Road, which indeed was in dire need of their services. This is not only untrue but unlikely since they did not know the city at all and lacked the antennae that northern nationalists claim to have as a built-in safety device. They had extreme difficulty in finding Chichester Street, then the home of Belfast's main fire station, and they were appalled at the extent of the destruction and by the bodies of dead humans and animals they had to pass on the way to it. Particularly severe even to the experienced firemen was the sight of lorries filled with corpses being taken to huge St George's Market near the Lagan where they would be laid out in the hope of identification.

One story from the time may, however, be true: as one rescue party removed house debris, hoping for signs of life, they were delighted to hear shouting from under the rubble. A family cowering under the stairs in the wreck of their house had been completely buried when the masonry collapsed on top of them and they had shouted until they were hoarse. Contact established, the officer in charge kept the survivors in chat and continued talking until the removal of brick and dust allowed them to see daylight and gingerly climb out. The father who had done the talking had noticed something unusual about the accents of the rescuers and did not recognise the uniforms. When asked who they were the firemen said, 'We're the Dublin Fire Brigade!' A typical Ulster crack followed: 'It must have been a mighty bomb to blow us from Belfast to Dublin.' Not all those who took refuge under their stairs were as fortunate. One Belfast AFS member, searching the remains of a wrecked house in York Street, opened a cupboard door to find an entire family, parents and three children, totally unmarked but dead from the effect of blast.

The Dubliners and fellow fire-fighters from the other Leinster towns fought the fires and helped dig for survivors all that Wednesday with no let-up and no food. There was no system of catering and few remaining shops to buy provisions even if they had had the cash. The Drogheda group assigned to the bottom of High Street, the area around the Albert Clock, came off best. The dockers and shipyard workers shared their 'pieces' with them as they went to work. The fare was not exactly from Fortnum and Mason – mainly door-stoppers of raw onion sandwiches washed down with milk – but it tasted heavenly. The crew members were later given five shillings each as compensation for their missed meals – a sum that at the time would buy them three slap-up 'tighteners' in eating-houses.

In spite of the nauseating and mounting horror there were lighter moments. A Dublin crew managed to hide their only mild disapproval when they saw looters remove stock from a pub in Chichester Street not far from headquarters. This opportunistic but entrepreneurial self-help continued even after the firemen started playing the hoses on the crumbling building. Undismayed the scavengers requested that the visitors cool down the bar's fiercely hot safe so that they could carry it off as well. Another Dubliner had been blithely running up and down a ladder as he played his hose on a burning building. His ladder had rested against the wall of the house and he was rather startled when the wall collapsed into rubble when the ladder was wheeled away. And like all good pieces of theatre the day ended with an element of farce. One of the Dublin tenders broke down and had to be towed home by a Dún Laoghaire pump.

It was a famous night and was long remembered; yet the details of how exactly the involvement of the southern crews came about are buried in a perhaps salutary and certainly deliberate obfuscation. There are a number of dramatis personae: Sir Basil Brooke, deputy prime minister of Northern Ireland; Major J.J. Comerford, Dublin's chief fire superintendent; R.D. Harrison, commissioner of the Royal Ulster Constabulary; P.J. Hernon, Dublin city manager; John MacDermott, Minister of Home Security in Northern Ireland; Cardinal Joseph MacRory (1861–1945) and, of course, de Valera. Details of telephone calls and telegram communication are sparse and contradictory.

The exact nature of the involvement of Cardinal MacRory is hard to sequence. He was known as the leader of the campaign against conscription and memories of his anti-Unionist stance during the pogroms of the early 1920s had made him known as a bitter and vocal enemy of the Stormont regime. The part he played in the sequence of the night's events is unclear since few documents survive. The likeliest possibility is that MacDermott appealed to him, as head of the Irish Church, resident in Armagh and unquestionably spiritual head of all Ireland, to intercede with de Valera to send aid. Though there is no record in either government's files of late-night communication it is more than likely that MacDermott was astute enough to use MacRory as a medium of communication. (MacRory later begged Hempel to use what influence he had to prevent the bombing of Armagh, the primatial city.)

It seems clear that MacDermott, on the advice of Harrison, decided to ask for help from the Éire fire service but with the same judicious caution that had him contact Brooke instead of the vacillating Andrews, probably used MacRory as his intermediary with de Valera. In his stern Unionist way, believing that the Free State was essentially priest-ridden, he probably expected that the cardinal could command de Valera to act against his will. For so astute a politician he had no real concept of relations between Church and State in the south. The process started around 1 am on Wednesday and by 2 am Comerford had arrived at Dublin's chief station in Tara Street with its elegant Florentine tower asking for volunteers to race to Belfast. He indicated in his request that it had come from the Taoiseach who had been speaking to 'the Primate'. Other sources suggest much the same sequence but place the timing as later by three hours, opining that MacDermott had not rung Brooke until 4.15 am and that a telegram was delivered to Hernon at 4.35 am. He logged a request by de Valera to 'give any assistance'. By 6.10 am Comerford was able to tell de Valera that the crews were on their way. There were questions about neutrality and more immediate concerns about insurance pointed out by Sean MacEntee the fiscally prudent Minister of Finance. Matters were eventually sorted out with the promise of retrospective legislation to cover any question of insurance.

It was the Dubliners' finest hour – northerners' knowledge of southern geography never precise enough to guess at the location of the other three 'D's. The papers reacted with their usual care with one eye on the censor. The *Irish Independent* of 17 April gave three columns to the Belfast Blitz but its only mention of the adventure was the single sentence: 'Units of fire-fighting and ambulance services from some of the towns in the Twenty-Six Counties assisted in putting out fires resulting from the raids.' The *Irish Press*, de Valera's own morning paper, barely mentioned the role of the southern appliances, and the *Herald* (the *Independent*'s evening paper) and its rival the *Evening Mail* (owned by *The Irish Times*) did not cover the story at all. Clearly the censor had visited all the newspaper offices. It was no wonder that the charismatic editor R.M. Smyllie (1894–1954), who reconciled *The Irish Times* to the Irish majority, in a fit of uncharacteristic restraint described the censors as 'troglyditic myrmidons, moronic clodhoppers, ignorant bosthoons, poor cawbogues whose only claim to literacy was their blue pencils'. It was a marvellous opportunity to collect the very best of human-interest stories and it was missed. Not one reporter interviewed the returning heroes. The *Irish Press* did eventually report de Valera's Castlebar speech on 19 April and the next day it was printed with approval in full by the Belfast *Northern Whig*.

Sixteen days later the fire fighters were in the news again for the same kind of reason. On the night of 5 May an air armada of 471 bombers left the *Luftwaffe* fields of northern

France with instructions to attack Liverpool, Barrow-in Furness (further north along the Lancashire coast) and Belfast. The Belfast contingent of 150 planes, mainly Heinkels and Dorniers, were given the task of starting a firestorm in the city and were armed for the purpose with 100,000 incendiary bombs and 220 tons of high explosives, dropped in units of 500 pounds. Conditions were perfect: a clear, still May night revealed the targets as clearly as on the bombardiers' maps, even though the planes stayed above the 7000-foot deployment of the barrage balloons. Within minutes the Great Fire of Belfast had begun; at the same time began the great exodus of civilians to go 'ditching' in the encircling hills.

This time Hernon kept a timed sequence of the events of the night jotted down on the back of an envelope. He was phoned by de Valera at 12.30 am to advise him that Belfast was being attacked again. 'Told me to be prepared to send assistance if called upon to do so.' De Valera rang fifteen minutes later to say that he would prefer that the appliances should travel by daylight but if an urgent call should come they were to 'take the risk and go'. By 2.25 am the urgency was established; de Valera told Hernon to send the teams, volunteers of course, but added a typical precise instruction: to confine their activities to 'rescue from private houses rather than military objectives'. By 3.40 am Comerford was able to tell Hernon that thirteen Dublin firemen had gone on two pumps and eleven others were about to take two further pumps. Dundalk, Drogheda and Dún Laoghaire each supplied one crew each and two further AFS crews had left Tara Street. In spite of this the chief fire officer in charge of the travellers, Superintendent Gorman, sent a telegram at 7 am: 'Fires out of control. Send seventeen men and one pump.'

When they returned home through the late May twilight, the firemen must have had some satisfaction after their part in a blistering experience in which they carried themselves with pride. They had helped both materially and morally, and for those who cared confirmed their countrymen's reputation for courage and generosity. They had learned much even about their own calling and discovered the hard way that Catholics and Protestants are indistinguishable in death from the skies. Deaths there were: fifteen in Belfast on 8 April during the industrial attack, in which the Dublin fire-fighters were not involved, though they could have been usefully employed; between nine hundred and a thousand people were killed and nearly as many seriously injured on the Easter Wednesday raid, in which most damage was inflicted on residential streets. The May air raid caused most strategic damage and fewer casualties among civilians, although at least a hundred and fifty were killed.

There was a general feeling of gratitude throughout the north towards the 'Free State firemen'. Faced with the sombre realisation that Heinkels and Dorniers had no absolute mechanism for distinguishing between Taigs and Prods, there followed a kind of lowering of sectarianism that persisted into the early 1950s. There were still hisses from the lunatic fringes on both sides. Some may literally have believed that the austere Pius XII flew in one of the German bombers directing their squadrons away from Catholic churches. These suffered less than the other many and varied edifices, called here for convenience non-Catholic, that were everywhere to be found in the city of God and noticed in each Saturday-evening edition of the *Belfast Telegraph* with a full broadsheet page detailing Sabbath services. St Matthew's Catholic church in Ballymacarret, near the shipyards, did have structural damage, as did Holy Family in Newington (the extent of the damage here discovered only years later during furbishment) but they were the only Catholic casualties. There were more than thirty places of Protestant worship razed to the ground or seriously in need of levelling. The extreme nationalists had made an issue of burning their gas-masks to show what they thought of ARP and were perhaps guilty as charged of using hand torches to direct the Luftwaffe on their missions.

A considerable advance in community relations was secured when Protestants from the Unionist Shankill and Catholics from the nearby Falls Road slept side by side in the cellars of the Redemptorist monastery of Clonard, which had been built on land between the two communities. They found that the people of other denominations had no horns, cloven hooves or tails. There was gratitude towards all the emergency services but towards the 'Staters' in particular.

MacDermott spoke about the work of the DFS and other services in Stormont on 22 April. His carefully worded statement summed up the general feeling:

> The help afforded by our Southern neighbours was not related to any bond of war or to any political consideration. It was above and beyond politics; it was based on a common humanity and we gratefully acknowledge it as such.

The *Irish News*, then as now the voice of constitutional nationalism, managed in an editorial to temper sincerity with political nous:

A word of high praise is due to the unstinted assistance given by our countrymen in the neutral part of this island to this area. Not only have they been prompt in sending their fire-fighting units, no trouble is too great for the citizens of Éire when it is a question of housing and sheltering refugees. Never was sympathy so manifest; never pity so practised. We in our day of sorrow thank our countrymen from the South.

A last word is due from the ultra-right-wing *Daily Telegraph*, never a friend of Ireland:

A wave of gratitude for Ireland's errand of mercy has swept the city of Belfast overnight, establishing a bond of sympathy between North and South Ireland which no British or Irish statesman has been able to establish in a generation.

The leader writer must have been feeling very euphoric indeed to have been lulled into using the word 'Ireland' instead of 'Éire' to refer to what had recently always been called the 'Free State'.

# 5

# 'It's a Bloody German Bomber Up There'

Northern Ireland was not attacked again; the autumn of 1941 saw the change in Axis tactics. Operation Sealion was aborted, yielding place to Barbarossa, the German grand strategy that would quickly conquer the USSR. The *Luftwaffe* had, it seemed, bigger fish to fry. Yet, scorpion-like, it had a sting in its tail that would startle the neutral island. There was a certain irony in that the most deadly visitation by the *Luftwaffe* in Ireland outside of Belfast should have been on Dublin.

Yet, as we have seen, there had been precedents. Though there had been much discussion, mainly hostile, in the areas where bombs fell and in government offices, Hempel had by now become inured to the frequent public protests and the slightly less embarrassing visits by officials from the Department of External Affairs. It was accepted diplomatically that the incidents in Carlow, Kildare, Drogheda and Dublin had resulted from error, although most people were certain that they were caused by the careless off-loading of superfluous armament. The minor Tuesday raid, the last on Belfast, was not, as we've seen, the last in Ireland. The *Derry Journal* carried a story on Friday, 7 May, deep in the lower recesses of page six. A bomb had been jettisoned at the farm of Patrick Douglas at Carthage Hill, Coolkenny, about nine miles from Malin Head, the most northerly point in Ireland, and two miles from the almost inaccessible fishing village of Glengad. It left a crater twenty-four feet in diameter and ten feet deep. Injuries were slight, Douglas receiving a few abrasions to his face. Protests made to Hempel at the legation were ignored but it was a kind of curtain-raiser for the greater fatality – a preview of the Dublin raid at the very end of the month of May. The capital was to experience its worst night since 1916 a mere twenty-three days after the Great Fire of Belfast.

It was Whit and Friday-night revellers were looking forward to an extended weekend. As Billy Cullen made his way home to his rooms in the tenement in Summerhill on Dublin's north side he was aware of the sound of an aeroplane. He could see the beams of the new searchlights that had recently been placed down at the docks lancing the sky. His unease grew as a plane with a limping sound was caught in cross-beams. Then he saw the black crosses that the *Luftwaffe* used as insignia on their planes and the swastikas on the tail, and ran back up the stairs, calling to his wife Mary to get dressed, wake the three children and take whatever cover they could. 'We'd better get out of here; it's a bloody German bomber up there!' Almost immediately they heard the crump of four bombs falling nearby and the sound of the plane immediately over their heads. Other tenants of the building came out of their rooms looking for reassurance and were comforted by Mary Cullen, who was the kind of person who took command in all emergencies. She told Billy she would see to her mother, Mrs Darcy, while he should go where he could be most useful. As he made his way along Summerhill towards Rutland Street school, the assembly place for ARP volunteers, he did his best to reassure the frightened people standing half-dressed in doorways that the danger was over and that the aircraft had gone away.

At the school he learned that the houses on both sides of the Newcomen Bridge over the Royal Canal had been flattened and that they were to make their way along Killarney Street to the Five Lamps, a well-known intersection in Ballybough. That Saturday night lived on in the memory of all who helped with the dead and wounded. By the time Billy Cullen and his team, headed by Captain Bolger, arrived at the main scene of the devastation the fire service had already arrived and the first job assigned to them was to cordon off the wide area of broken houses, deep craters and exposed drains and wiring. Billy and his companions worked for more than eighteen hours digging out the ruined bodies of people they knew, some headless, some without legs. Billy Cullen's son, Bill, described the event, often retold by his father, in his autobiography, *It's a Long Way from Penny Apples* (2001) and though it is relegated almost to a footnote in histories of the time it was a cataclysm never forgotten in that tight community of north inner Dublin.

In all four bombs were dropped, the first, estimated to have weighed 250 pounds, fell at the junction of the North Circular Road and North Richmond Street, close to the O'Connell's Christian Brothers School. It demolished No 582 North Circular Road, a shop, trapping the occupants under the debris, and set the house next door on fire. The emergency services were on the scene very quickly and they were able to extricate them, still alive but injured. The Dublin Fire Service from Dorset Street station was able to extinguish the flames with the same dispatch but they were concerned that water, gas and electricity mains were damaged and sewers exposed. The LDF and LSF, also on the scene, helped with the work of clearing the rubble and forming safety cordons to keep back the curious and frightened crowds of people who had gathered. Neighbouring houses had suffered collateral damage, with roofs torn off and windows blown in.

It was while the emergency services were coping admirably with the damage that the fourth, much larger bomb, fitted with a grisly whistle to add to the terror, landed at another junction, the intersection of North William Street (that ran south from Summerhill Parade) and North Strand Road just beside the Newcomen Bridge over the Royal Canal. It was then 2.05 am. From the fragments gathered at the scene the experts were able to say that it had been a 500-pound high explosive bomb. The tramlines were twisted into a horrible knot and eleven houses on one side of the street were completely demolished. The buildings levelled included a butcher's shop, a pork store, a jeweller's and a greengrocery. An equal number of houses on the other side suffered the same fate.

In all twenty-five houses were completely demolished and forty-five others had to be razed, as no longer fit for habitation. Three hundred dwellings were declared 'temporarily unfit for dwelling', while the most appalling aspect of the situation was the condition of the casualties as they were dragged from the ruins of their homes. Morphine was used to ease the pain of those trapped and for those still out of reach, tea and soup were fed to them by long tubes. Forty-five people were seriously injured and taken to hospital while up to three hundred were treated on the spot for minor injuries by the Irish Red Cross and the St John Ambulance Service. Surviving children, terrified and unbelieving, ran screaming in their night attire about the nightmarish confusion that a few moments before had been their place of security. Seventeen bodies had been recovered by ten o'clock on the Saturday evening and the final toll of fatalities, as reported by the Department of Defence on 8 July, was eight men, ten women, seven children and two unidentified bodies. These, according to the department, were 'killed outright'.

The firemen, troops, ARP workers and LSF units were joined by able-bodied men from the district. Like Billy Cullen they worked through the day, pulling out the bodies of the dead and the dying, relieved to find some neighbours still alive if badly hurt. The second bomb had fallen in Summerhill Parade, less than 200 yards away from the first, demolishing two houses, Nos 43 and 44. The third fell in Phoenix Park at the pumping station by the Dog Pond. It badly damaged one house but the occupants, a man and his daughter, escaped with only minor injuries. It had fallen close enough to Áras an Uachtaráin to blast out the windows and terrified the animals in the Zoological Gardens.

The injured were taken to the Mater in Eccles Street and other local hospitals and the number of dead, reckoned first as twenty-nine, taken to mortuaries in the same buildings. That total would be added to as more bodies were discovered and some of the most seriously hurt succumbed to their injuries. The fire service extinguished any residual pockets of fire as a matter of urgency because they had been alerted to the danger of explosions by officials of the city gas company, who were busy cutting off supplies. The fact that no incendiaries were dropped and that all the fires that the service had to deal with were caused by the collapse of the slum housing was a clear indication that no punitive air raid was intended. The Belfast experience in the May raid was that fire did much more damage than high explosive.

All the rescue services, statutory and volunteer, helped tend to the dazed people shocked and wandering about in the side streets and laneways. The city morgue and local hospitals, especially the Mater, were crowded with anxious relatives and friends hoping to have their worst fears allayed. What was clear to all the rescue workers was the poor quality of the houses and the depredation that one bomb could cause. It was the Dublin equivalent of the Belfast experience when rows of houses collapsed in a ghastly domino effect. Three hundred Dublin dwellings were flattened or effectively rendered into heaps of rubble. Blast damage can be powerful and far-reaching, as one later event was to prove. The firemen coming on fresh watch joined their mates on the night shift and all firefighters on leave for the Whit weekend were recalled to duty. It was not until Saturday afternoon that the men on the night watch were stood down and allowed to go home.

The city council and the local papers eventually published a list of the fatalities and the places where they were buried. The seven members of the Browne family, ranging in age from Angela, who was two, to Granny Mary Browne, aged seventy-five, who had lived in 24 North Strand Road were interred in Edenderry, County Offaly, their native place. Further along the street at No 28, the four Fitzpatricks, father Richard (66), mother Ellen (55) and twins Madge and Noel (32) as native Dubliners were buried in Glasnevin, as were John Murray and Mrs Marion Horton of No 156. These funerals took place on Wednesday, 4 June. That same day Charles Sweeney of 11 North Strand Road and Mrs Mary Ellen

Boyle of No 157 were buried in Deansgrange on the other side of the city. Twelve others were given a public funeral on the following day, all but one from North Strand Road. Two of them were unidentified but it was known that they lived in a tenement, No 157. The rest were members of the Foran family of No 155, the Fitzpatricks of 156 across the street, Thomas Carroll and his daughter Mrs Josephine Fagan, who lived next door to the Forans, Patrick Callely and Elizabeth Daly also of No 162 and William McLaughlin, the two-year-old son of Patrick McLaughlin whose home address was at 41 Summerhill. (Unfortunately for them they had spent the night at 157 North Circular Road and were caught in the explosion. Patrick's remains were not found until 9 June. Lily Behan who had lived at 72 Shelmalier Road some distance apart from the main target died of her injuries nearly three months later on 22 August.)

The public funeral on Thursday 5 June was attended by de Valera and other members of the government. The Mass in the Church of St Laurence O'Toole in Seville Place was presided over by John Charles McQuaid (1895–1973) who had been consecrated archbishop the previous November. This church on the eastern side of the Great Northern Railway line was the nearest undamaged one to the scene of the bombings. The dead were then taken to Glasnevin Cemetery in twelve hearses.

That afternoon de Valera spoke in the Dáil associating all the members with the sympathy already expressed by the government:

> Although a complete survey has not yet been
> possible, the latest report which I have received

is that twenty-seven were killed outright or subsequently died; forty-five were wounded or received other serious bodily injury and are still in hospital; twenty-five houses were completely destroyed and three hundred so damaged as to be unfit for habitation, leaving many hundreds of people homeless.

He went on to praise:

...the several voluntary organisations the devoted exertions of whose members helped to confine the extent of the disaster and have mitigated the sufferings of those affected by it. As I have already informed the public, a protest has already been made to the German government. The Dáil will not expect me, at the moment, to say more on this head.

Chief among the voluntary organisations was the Irish Red Cross, which commandeered the Mansion House in Dawson Street as a shelter for the dispossessed; other public buildings were used as well. The shock composed as much of disbelief as of fear and misery took some time to diminish.

Shocking as the Dublin raid was the death toll was slight compared to that in Belfast on the Tuesday night and Wednesday morning of Easter week when 745 were killed. In the month of May 1941, in Britain as a whole, 5394 people died and this when the Blitz was beginning to peter out. Also ironical was the fact that the two planes that caused all the destruction were on their way back to base, having failed to find suitable conditions for bombing Belfast. An even bigger irony and one that gave all but Fianna Fáil supporters a great deal of glee tempered with regrets for the deceased, concerned the affair of Old Bride Street. Four columns in from the left on the front page of *The Irish Times* of Monday, 2 June, overshadowed by the heavy black main headline 'German Bombs Were Dropped on Dublin', was a story headed 'Dublin Houses Collapse' followed by the sub-head: 'Three Persons Killed.'

Two houses collapsed and a third partially fell in Old Bride Street just after 10 o'clock on the Sunday morning, 1 June. The dead all lived at No 46 (described in the *Times* as a tenement house) that was effectively derelict. Mrs Lynskey, aged thirty, had been given the key of a new house at Kimmage, part of a Dublin Corporation rehousing scheme, and was due to leave on the Tuesday. She, her five-month-old baby Noel and a pensioner Samuel O'Brien, aged seventy-two, who used to work in Guinness's Brewery died immediately.

Old Bride Street has since disappeared, replaced by much needed redevelopment in the environs of St Patrick's Cathedral, but the age and frailty of these buildings should already have made clear that urgent demolition was necessary. These houses were about a mile and a half from the site of the North Strand bomb and it is more than likely that they were badly shaken by blast damage, which was delayed in its effect for thirty hours. It was reported that they collapsed shortly after a heavy lorry had passed down the narrow street. Whatever the final cause, the dwellings in Old Bride Street that crumbled and the unlucky occupants must be regarded as further, although accidental, casualties of the events of the Saturday morning.

Dublin Corporation officials wisely evacuated the nearest buildings on Old Bride Street and arranged for twenty-nine occupants of the neighbouring houses to receive temporary accommodation at Red Cross headquarters at Mespil Road, while others stayed with relatives and friends in the district. There were sixty officials on duty and they already had the unenviable task of placing the 441 refugees from the North Strand Road whose dwellings had been declared unsafe by wardens or Corporation officials. The Old Bride Street affair acted as a ghastly counterpoint to the main disaster: a story that would under normal circumstances have been given top billing was relegated to a secondary position.

The *Times* reporter was able to talk to one of the survivors of the collapse, the fifteen-year-old Patrick Hanvey, who lived at No 47, next door, and whose family kept a small cycle-repair shop. He was a member of the ARP Emergency Communications Service, useful since cyclists could get through with messages when other means had failed. His main concern was to protect his blue uniform helmet. He said that he woke at ten o'clock to find pieces of the wall falling down and he was able to alert the other members of the Hanvey family, his parents and his five siblings, who all escaped without injury. A number of people were trapped and though the Tara Street fire brigade arrived within minutes they needed more help to dig out survivors from the rubble. An ARP rescue service was summoned from North Strand Road where they had been helping clear the much greater accumulation of rubble at the bomb site. George Leigh, one of the firemen, was overcome by gas from a broken main as he wriggled his way through a small gap in the debris to rescue Mrs Georgina O'Brien, who was also suffering the effects of gas inhalation. Both were treated at the Adelaide Hospital and later discharged.

There was general regret at the three deaths, particularly that of Mrs Lynskey, who was about to start a new life in Kimmage. It was noted by sociologists, amateur and otherwise, that the thirteen people, who lived in No 46 constituted several families: Atkinsons, O'Briens, Doyles, Lawlors and Lynskeys. They were comforted by Fr Walsh, a Carmelite, from the nearby church in Whitefriar Street and he visited the injured in the Adelaide Street and Meath Hospitals. He and the Adelaide doctors had waited by the site in case they could have been of assistance, spiritual and corporal. Members of the LSF also stood there employed to keep away from the site, the inevitable crowd of spectators who showed the same mixture of curiosity and trepidation that characterised the greater crowds who had assembled by Newcomen Bridge and the Royal Canal.

There incredulity and fear had given way to interest and speculation. There was also an odd formality about the procedures. Whenever a broken corpse was taken out of the rubble the guards and men of the emergency services, fire fighters, wardens, members of the LSF saluted, while the women of the Red Cross and St John Ambulance Service stood to attention. The agony was long-drawn-out as missing persons were finally confirmed as dead. The seven bodies of the Browne family, who had come to Dublin from Edenderry in County Offaly were identified by John Corrigan, the father of Mrs Mary Corrigan, the mother of the family. Four members of the Fitzpatrick family – the father and mother, son Noel and daughter Madge – were identified by the remaining surviving children, Mona and Gerard.

One kindly light amid the encircling gloom was the news that 100 houses, in the Cabra area, not due to be completed for three weeks, were being worked upon non-stop by electricians, plumbers and carpenters to have them ready for instant occupation. One memory of a child, then eight and a half, who lived in Phibsborough near where the bombs fell, was of the slightly comic reaction to the events of that Saturday morning. That evening there were queues for Confession in St Peter's Church that stretched out of the building and right round the corner of the Cabra Road and she could not help but notice that most of the penitents were men.

# 6

## AFTER THE RAID

On the Sunday night a government statement was rushed to press offices, partly as reassurance but mainly to demonstrate its measured anger at what may not have been intended as a 'raid' at all. The official statement read:

> The government regrets to announce that as a result of the bombs dropped on Dublin during the early hours of Saturday morning at least twenty-seven people lost their lives and about eighty received injuries. A further bomb was dropped near Arklow this morning. No lives were lost but there was some damage to property.
>
> Investigations having shown that the bombs dropped were of German origin, the Chargé d'Affaires in Berlin is being directed to protest, in the strongest terms, to the German Government against the violation of Irish territory, and to claim compensation and reparation for the loss of life and the damage to property. He is being further directed to ask for definite assurances that the strictest instructions will be given to

prevent the flight of aircraft over Irish territory and territorial waters.

The government in a second message also offered sympathy on behalf of the whole nation with all those who had been bereaved or had suffered injury or loss in the bombing. It concluded:

> The Government wishes also to express its appreciation of the splendid services rendered by the Garda, ARP organisations, LSF, the first-aid medical services and in particular the Red Cross and St John Ambulance Brigade, and the staffs of the city hospitals, who gave such devoted care to the injured.

The Arklow 'raid', coming so soon after the carnage in Dublin, seemed hardly worth mentioning. The skies of Leinster were full of *Luftwaffe* aircraft and that Saturday night and Sunday morning a red alert was issued again for the city. Inland observer posts in Waterford, Wexford, Kilkenny, Carlow, Offaly, Laois, Kildare and Westmeath reported aircraft in the hardly darkened night sky. From 2357 the number of planes coming from the south-east and flying north seemed to suggest that another raid on Dublin was imminent. Continuous waves of bombers were tracked flying north between midnight and 0042 and continuous explosions were heard between midnight and 2 am but none fell on the city. The explosions that seemed to be off-shore were undoubtedly caused by planes turning and dumping but LOP 9 at Wicklow Head reported one bright flash and a loud explosion in the direction of Arklow. The town, a fishing port and popular seaside resort, is about thirteen miles south south-west of the observation post. (The *Belfast News-Letter* in its report on Monday, 2 June helpfully added '[Note: Arklow is in County Wicklow.]' The emergency was declared over at 0400 and damage assessed at some broken windows; there was no loss of life.

The voluntary services had indeed done well at all four sites and at the Old Bride Street collapse that they wisely treated as a further victim of the bombs. When the Belfast fire service heard of the bombing, conscious of the help they had received seven weeks earlier, they immediately offered to drive down with reciprocal aid. Comerford was able to reassure them that their generously offered help was appreciated but not required. In comparison to the Belfast raids there were no serious fires since no fire bombs were dropped. The Dublin defence forces had done a remarkably efficient job.

One theory, proposing that the destruction had been a kind of punishment for Éire's not being neutral enough, seeming to be more partial to Britain than Germany, was that the intended targets were, in order, the fire stations of North Strand and Dorset Street and Áras an Uachtaráin. The suggestion came from Leo Sheridan after research in Germany and he added that the bombs were to be carried by a single Dornier Do17. Sheridan's *Irish Times* article (19 June 1997) was countered by Michael Kennedy in his book *Guarding Neutral Ireland,* Kennedy insisting that two or more German bombers were involved and that they were on their way back south after having failed to find a target in Belfast. Kennedy makes a strong case that, as on many other occasions, the bombardiers were jettisoning their heavy and dangerous cargo because of shortage of fuel. Kennedy's conclusions are based upon study of the reports of the many LPOs that were involved that Saturday morning.

Kennedy's version seems the most likely and it is worthwhile giving it in some detail. He rejects the propositions that Dublin was the intended target or that it was mistaken for Belfast. At 2340 on the night of 30 May, LOP 15 located at Forlorn Point on the south Wexford coast, close to Kilmore Quay and opposite the Saltees, reported unidentified aircraft over Irish territory. It, like its neighbours Carnsore Point, Greenore Point and Ballyconnigar Hill to the north and east and Hook Head, Brownstone Head, Dunabrattin Head in County Waterford to the west, was regularly aware of German planes who used the Irish coast as a convenient route up the Irish Sea. Eight minutes later an air-raid warning, coded 'yellow', was issued and the ack-ack crews and searchlight companies were 'stood up'. A second wave of 'bandits' passed over Carnsore Point at 0034. Aircraft were tracked at Mullingar and Portarlington, and were over Mountrath, County Laois at 0041. It was assumed that the planes were about to give Belfast another pounding. It was the first wave of these tracked going steadily north that was beginning to cause the watchers some concern. Wicklow Head alerted LOP 8 at Bray Head and a code 'red' was issued. Contrary to cinematic usage searchlights did not sweep the sky but were switched on and off as required; they made too easy a target. The few ack-ack guns were loaded and maximum projectile angles set but the planes of the first wave flew on over the city.

The alert continued for more than two hours when they were observed flying south again and seeming again to menace Dublin. At 0035 the Clontarf AA battery found an enemy plane in its sights and fired four rounds. It was rocked out of its flight path and that seemed to suggest that it was heading away from Dublin with the intention of releasing its bombs harmlessly into the Irish Sea as so many had been doing for weeks. Two 'large twin-engined monoplanes' coming from the north were fired on between 0128 and 0131 by batteries at Ringsend, Clontarf, Stillorgan and Ballyfermot. Then the bombs began to fall. It was established that the plane or planes that dropped the lethal bombs had not been fired at, thus refuting the argument by a pro-German lobby that the bombs were dropped in self-defence. As we have seen the really hard-line anti-British section of the population were absolutely convinced that the raid had been carried out by the RAF. They were not shaken out of this belief by the evidence from bomb fragments that proved to be German. It was still the RAF that was to blame, this time cleverly using captured German bombs. When Department of Defence reports proved that the bombers were Dorniers and Heinkels, recognisable to the sound locators by the intermittent engine sound, the answer from the sceptics was that RAF pilots were flying German planes.

Strangely Hempel, after his first shock, tried a similar excuse. He suggested that the bombing had been done by the British in captured German planes with the purpose of getting Ireland into the war. Their line, he suggested, would be: 'Oh look what the Germans have done!' Walshe summoned him to his office and asked him to explain. (Walshe acted, of course, on de Valera's instructions.) Hempel did not believe that the bombing could have been deliberate and he had already warned Berlin not to use the events for any propaganda purposes. He agreed with Walshe that the regular overflights by *Luftwaffe* had not helped improve relations with Ireland and this latest episode had 'done nothing but harm'. The German authorities reassured William Warnock, the Irish chargé d'affaires, that there would be widespread investigations and examination of all parties concerned and then if necessary reparations would be paid. This represented a change in the official attitude. At first in a statement on 5 June the Germans boldly asserted that the bombing of Dublin 'was a provocative act by the British. The discovery of bomb splinters is not conclusive proof because there have been other cases in which bombs seized as booty have been used for such purposes.' The spokesman had a sufficient grasp of reality to add:

> Our standpoint, which we made clear, is that it is naturally absurd to suggest that a German plane intentionally bombed Dublin and other towns in Éire. If bombs were dropped from a German plane it is obvious that the German airman must have thought he was over another city. There is always the possibility, however, that it was provocative bombing by other quarters. The fact that German bomb splinters were found is no proof that they were dropped by a German plane since the British undoubtedly possess captured German bombs just as we have captured British bombs. A strict enquiry into the incident is now taking place in order to ascertain whether there were German aircraft in the area at the time when the bombs were dropped.

The wilder speculators had, of course, a field day. Even sober citizens could recall having heard that Lord Haw-Haw had named Amiens Street station, where Belfast refugees from their Blitz alighted from the GNR train, as a target. In fact the station was hardly half a mile from the Newcomen Bridge. The same broadcast was reported to have said that Dundalk was also a legitimate target because it was the port of export for Irish cattle to England. As if on cue (though essentially bad theatre) between 0130 hours and 0132 on 24 July, George's Quay in Dundalk was bombed. The attack included at least one large high explosive bomb but there were no casualties and only minor damage was inflicted. In spite of Joyce's forewarning, this 'raid' had all the marks of a careless dumping of explosive ballast after an unsuccessful sortie. The Irish Sea and the Irish coast were blanketed by large formations of German aircraft all that month of July 1941 and there were many yellow alerts and some red. It was, however, the last time that any threat of *Luftwaffe* raids was present.

# 7

# It Said in the Papers

The papers were full of genuine sympathy for the bereaved but inevitably betrayed a political element in their editorials. *The Derry Journal* headed its leader of Monday, 2 June 1941 'Casualties in the Cause of Peace' and expatiated on the nationalist North's debt to 'the Government and people of the Irish State for making common cause with us against the threat of conscription.' (The paper was always adamant about its correct use of topographical description. It could never bring itself to use the word 'Ulster', unless accurately to describe the nine counties. Even abbreviations such as the 'U'TA ('Ulster' Transport Authority) or 'U'TV ('Ulster' Television) were given the mockingly subjective quotation marks. And it could never bring itself to use the form 'Éire', insisting upon the 'Irish State'.) Now, it continued, 'we have reason to grieve with them.'

The leader wisely decided not to exaggerate the scale of the occurrence or to equate it to an organised raid – 'an all too ghastly a feature of this war'. The severe bombings of Belfast a month and half earlier were still clear in the minds of the staff and Derry itself had experienced two land mines that floated gently down to kill fifteen people on the Wednesday of Easter Week. The author of the piece came down (as with the Derry raid) on the side of navigational error:

> While those conversant with the terrible technique of night bombing could explain how in aerial navigation a margin of error could occur, if such can be the explanation, it is much harder to conceive of any motive which would put a still graver complex on the matter.

It was a typical example of playing safe within the rules of censorship but also of pleasing the wide spectrum of the *Journal*'s readership from extreme republicanism to a mild form of Catholic Unionism. Germany could no more be attacked than Britain be praised. Éire's neutral stance was, of course, admirable and the victims of the bombings were innocent and even heroic. The peroration was a masterly example of Orwellian Newspeak, seven years before *Nineteen Eighty-four* was published:

> The lives of those who have perished in such shocking circumstances are part of the sacrifice incurred in the struggle of the Irish State to ward off greater evils. Let us look upon Dublin's trials in this light while we pray for those who have made the supreme sacrifice, for peace, that perpetual light may shine upon them. *Go ndeannaidh Dia trócaire ar a n-anam.*

The *Journal*'s coverage of the bombing had details more colourful and more grisly than the other northern papers. Mary

Dempsey, whose house in 26 North Strand Road crumpled around her, was able to struggle out of her bedroom window, place a roof ladder on the rubble and rescue her mother, who was also unhurt. The newspaper mentions at least three decapitations: a headless body of a man on the pavement of North Strand Road and two bodies 'completely decapitated' discovered in the same house by a Dr J.C. Wauch, who had come to help.

In the Tuesday's *Londonderry Sentinel* the editorial had the same topic, yet with a subtle change of emphasis. (The *Journal* was published on Mondays, Wednesdays and Fridays; the *Sentinel* on Tuesdays, Thursdays and Saturdays.) As one of two Unionist papers in the city it was strongly pro-British and Germany was the enemy. It began by noting that:

> Although bombs have been dropped on neutral Éire on a number of occasions by German airmen since the war began the loss of life, the number of injured, the destruction of property and the circumstances were in no way comparable with those of Saturday morning's raid. In all earlier bomb-dropping the casualties were few and the damage not great. On Saturday over thirty people were killed and almost a hundred injured; twenty houses were completely destroyed and more than fifty damaged, resulting in many people being rendered homeless. Apart from the bombs dropped on Dublin last January it is possible to conceive that the Nazi airmen had made navigational errors and were unaware of where they were.

They went on to voice what was in most people's minds: Dublin was not blacked out; an interval of more than half an hour elapsed between the dropping of the first bomb and the last; during that interval the airmen 'can hardly have failed to realise that they were over neutral territory'. It pointed out that there were no RAF planes in pursuit and that the few shells fired by Dublin's ack-ack defences hardly provided an excuse. In its news coverage the *Sentinel* noted that the death-roll was now thirty-three and, as was perfectly proper for a provincial paper, recorded the death 'as a result of Saturday morning's bombing in Dublin' of Charles Sweeney, a Derryman, who had been stationmaster in Ballyliffin and Carndonagh, head clerk to the Londonderry and Lough Swilly Railway and afterwards stationmaster in Dunkineely for the County Donegal Railway. Sincerest sympathy was offered to 'his bereaved widow and family and to his relatives here in Londonderry in their tragic sorrow'. Sweeney was one of the late-listed, dying of his injuries in the Richmond Hospital on the Sunday morning.

The third Derry paper, the *Standard*, tended in peacetime to represent Presbyterianism and it also strongly backed the war effort. Its editorial printed on Monday, 2 June was headed 'Neutrality No Safeguard'. Its comment about the 'strong protest to Berlin' was to dismiss it as worthless:

> Will any self-respecting government or country regard the sternest protest sufficient in the circumstances, even if Germany should offer a humble apology and promise adequate compensation? It will be recalled that on a previous occasion when German bombs fell on Éire the German wireless

declared that these bombs were either British or imaginary. We also have some recollection that on another occasion the Nazis denied an attack upon Éire an hour or so before it materialised.

All is fair in war at least. The writer was adamant that the element of accident should immediately be ruled out as 'not sustainable'. He also considered excuses that the Nazis 'with their usual ingenuity' may invent. He dismissed the possibility that the attack was made by British planes. 'There is no one in Ireland, including even the Germans and Italians in neutral Éire itself, who would for a moment give serious heed to such an assertion.' (It is remarkable how much visceral disapproval can be packed into an apparently innocent sentence.) Having at somewhat repetitive length – and to his own satisfaction – proved Germany's guilt he goes on to speculate about the 'reaction in Éire'. In spite of declaring general sympathy for the injuries and loss of life the editorial cannot resist a kind of teasing about inconsistencies in de Valera's attitudes. He recalls 'some of Mr de Valera's reiterated statements' that Éire would not be used as a base for an attack upon Britain by any other country in the world and that if any of the belligerents attacked her Éire would fight to retain her independence. 'There was no exception made in the case of an attack by air.' It was almost with a kind of satisfaction that he intended to 'watch the developments that such a very serious onslaught upon a helpless Dublin must inevitably create'.

The leading Belfast morning, the *News-Letter*, founded in 1737, making it Belfast first and Ireland's oldest newspaper, carried the story on page six but gave it twenty column-inches, a straightforward account of the events as known. Its edition of Saturday 31 May had carried a few inches under the heads 'Bombs Dropped in Dublin', 'Raid Lasts Half an Hour' and 'Great Fire Raging'. It was a story it had picked up from the wires and lacked a deal of accuracy and completeness. There was not 'a heavy anti-aircraft barrage' – the Defence Forces could not afford that luxury; searchlights did not sweep the sky – they were turned on and off to avoid being a target and there was no 'great fire raging' – and no incendiaries were dropped. The story had a 'boxed' note in the middle headed 'Raiders over Ulster' giving a joint communiqué from the Northern Ireland Ministry of Public Security and RAF Headquarters: 'During the hours of darkness some enemy aircraft crossed over into Northern Ireland. No incidents have been reported.' It was a non-story, a piece of required publication, but the enemy aircraft that crossed over into Northern Ireland have been a contributory factor to the bombs that later fell in Dublin. The Monday account, with more space available, drew attention to the fact that 'the windows of Dr Hyde's residence were smashed and windows were smashed also in the American Legation'. The official name of 'Dr Hyde's residence' was then beyond the ingenuity of the *News-Letter*'s typesetters.

(To be fair the *Irish News* of the same date did attempt to use the Irish title but its version had two typographical errors. It, true to its background, singled out for special commendation the Sisters of Charity of St Vincent de Paul who 'throughout the night worked unceasingly with the Red Cross workers in looking after the hundreds of people who were housed at the convent.')

The *News-Letter* alone of all the Ulster papers carried the story that the bison in the Zoological Gardens in the Phoenix Park smashed the heavy railings of its enclosure. (The

*Northern Whig*, Belfast's slightly more radical morning paper, carried the story on Monday 1 June, with the now all too familiar detail, using the almost inevitable subhead 'Family Wiped Out' but its particular slant was that at the Zoological Gardens 'firing squads stood by to shoot the animals should it be necessary.')

The *News-Letter*'s closing paragraph carried the story of the Belfast fire fighters offer and ended with a characteristic, slightly dubious concern for Éire's status:

> As soon as news of the outrage reached Belfast the authorities offered to send detachments of the Fire Brigade to Dublin, but the Éire authorities, while appreciating the offer, said that they could cope with the situation. This was the eighth occasion on which German aircraft have dropped bombs on neutral Éire.

One of the few bright aspects of the eight occasions on which bombings occurred was the rapidity of response, efficiency and general kindness of the various emergency agencies – rescue, medical, religious and welfare. It was with no sense of bravado that the Dublin fire and rescue services turned down the Belfast offer. On that occasion – and it was thankfully the last – there was no need for outside assistance, although the offer was greatly appreciated.

The *Belfast Telegraph* as an evening paper was able to carry a fuller version of the story on 31 May and consequently had a much shorter list of known dead, twenty-two, with thirty unaccounted for. It also carried on its banner the reminder that it was the 271st day of the war's second year. One of its human-interest stories concerned Gerald Fitzpatrick of 28 North Strand Road, who arrived home after a dance to find the house demolished, his father and mother dead and his brother and sister missing. In fact the missing siblings were the twins Madge and Noel who were buried in Glasnevin on Wednesday, 4 June, along with their parents. Another sad case was that of Patrick Boyle who, after the first bomb ran round to check that his mother was safe and returned to find that his wife and child were missing. Among the list of those buried at Deansgrange on Wednesday, 4 June, was Mrs Mary Ellen Boyle of 127 North Strand Road. There is no information about the missing child. On a cheerier note the *Belfast Telegraph* told of a man who had been trapped by debris in his bed. The first thing he asked for when rescued by first-aid workers was a cigarette. Other word pictures in the *Telegraph*'s coverage included the remark of Dr Danahar, house surgeon at Jervis Street, commenting in the male chauvinistic way characteristic of the time that the spirit of the people was remarkably good:

> Even the women amongst the injured behaved calmly and with great courage and restraint. There were few scenes of hysteria, which made it easier to exercise discipline over the injured so that the more seriously injured could be taken first.

The paper told of a young priest crawling over the debris, comforting the injured and badly wounded: 'His clothes were covered with grime and dust.'

The *Irish News* of Saturday, 6 June was concerned with Berlin's response to Warnock's 'handed-in' note to the German

Foreign Office. It gave two alternative explanations: the first that the Dublin bombing was a provocative act by the British, the second that if the bombs were dropped by German planes, the act was not intentional. It added: 'A strict inquiry into the incident is now taking place in order to ascertain whether it was possible for a German plane to have dropped the bombs – that is to say whether there were German aircraft in the area at the time.'

The paper gave some more detail about the public funeral of victims on Sunday, 5 June. There were twelve hearses led by the Garda band with immediate relatives following behind. De Valera and the Speaker of the Dáil, Frank Fahy, were accompanied by members of both Dáil and Seanad and large contingents of the LDF, the LSF, AFS, St John's Ambulance and the Red Cross. Their route lay through 'the devastated portion of the North Strand, where many of the victims met their untimely end. The remains of two unidentified victims were interred in the same grave.'

The Dublin dailies carried as much of the story as they thought judicious, conscious as ever of the hot breath of the censor at their backs. There was not much variation in the editorials. The *Irish Press* headed its leader 'The Dublin Bombing' and looking for a positive angle insisted that 'this awful tragedy has also had its noble side' noting that 'throughout the last two days and nights the courage and devotion of their [the emergency services] members have been superb. Lives were willingly risked that life might be saved…and in so far as this great calamity could be softened gallantry, kindliness and noble actions alleviated it. Its final paragraph rehearsed the need for continuing watchfulness:

> ...we trust that Irishmen in every part of the country will now realise the immense value of careful preparation for any sudden crisis that may arise, and will push forward the work of organising and perfecting themselves in the various tasks they have to undertake.

The peroration re-echoes the public sympathy that all public agencies had stated: 'We join too with the government in offering our deep sympathy to those who have suffered in this cruel tragedy.'

The *Irish Independent* with its heading 'Bombs on Dublin' like its two sisters emphasised the meticulous correctness of the Irish government's handling of neutrality. They also shared an expectancy that Germany would respond positively to the Irish protests not only in the matter of reparations but in the reassurances demanded and awaited... 'we have every right to make the protest that is being presented and to expect that the undertakings sought will be unhesitatingly given and carried out.'The writer used the opportunity to draw attention to the fact that the Irish Red Cross Society and the St John Ambulance Brigade had issued a joint appeal for funds and he expected from the readers 'a quick and large-hearted response'. The *Independent* leader closed with the common optimistic view that 'even this black tragedy is lightened by the heroism and sacrifice of those who have undertaken the patriotic duty of protecting, helping and comforting the populace.'

The *Times*'s leader replicated the news it carried on its front page but was the only one to note the extra sadness that 'nearly all the victims belonged to the poorer classes of Dublin's citizens, and the scenes witnessed as dawn was breaking on Saturday morning were indescribably tragic. No praise would be too high for the people who joined in the work of rescue and of succour to the wounded, many of whom were women and little children.'

It was a matter of no surprise that the content and the opinions expressed should have been so similar. The heading for the Times's leader was 'Death by Night', the most dramatic of the three, but it was not a time for disagreement nor for the usual political points-scoring. The staff of the papers were as shocked, bewildered, angry and scared as the rest of the populace. The leaders reflected the predominant emotion of incredulity that such a thing could have happened. The final effect was to the advantage of Fianna Fáil, the party in government, but not even the crankiest of extremists suggested that de Valera had rigged it for that purpose. Most of the 'don't-knows' were won over and Fine Gael, the opposition party, might then have agreed to serve in a government of national unity such as had existed in Britain since Chamberlain. All speculation about the future proved vain as always; politicians could not have known that the north-city raid was to be the last, not only in the city but in the country as a whole. Three years later the war still occupied the main stories on the front pages. *The Irish Times* of 2 June 1941 told how the Germans had captured Crete; the edition of 6 June 1944 told of the ten miles' advance of the Allies into France.

8

# The Reason Why

It was not long after the Whitsun raid that people began to wonder why for no apparent reason Dublin civilians should have died and houses of no tactical value – indeed of little value of any kind – should have been destroyed. The cranks advanced their far-fetched theories, usually against the old enemy, but only those with the same tunnel vision assented. There were, as with earlier raids, three sequential charges, each following the previous one as it was proved untenable. The first was the most simplistic and least likely: the bombs had been dropped by RAF planes as anti-German propaganda; the second that the RAF had dropped German bombs and the third that RAF pilots flying German planes had been responsible. The suggestion that RAF planes carried out the raid collapsed when LOP reports could place no British planes anywhere near Dublin that night and it was established from the fragments that the bombs were of German manufacture. That demolished the first two convenient theories that the Brits did it and that they used German bombs in their own bombers.

The third strongly held alternative belief was that the British used a captured *Luftwaffe* plane to drop captured

German bombs on Dublin. No one could explain how this capture of these German high explosives was effected, especially since virtually the whole of Europe was in the hands of the Axis powers. This theory was disproved by the presence in Irish airspace at the time of many German planes. The idea was, however, a convenient, not to say an attractive one, and it was offered at the beginning by the startled German representative Eduard Hempel, who had never quite got used to explaining away the often reprehensible actions of his masters. His diplomatic staff was not always diplomatic, tending to a kind of triumphalist arrogance when Germany was at the height of its powers. The Irish government, getting a trifle weary of reiterated statements and denials, were sure that the bombs and their carriers were both *echt Deutsch*.

The source of the raid having been established, the questions became more insistent and more difficult. Was the North Strand bombing unintentional or deliberate? The answers about the earlier raids had not been very satisfactory. Three deaths at Campile, though by British standards insignificant, seemed pointlessly cruel, and the damage to the creamery and the railway at Duncormick and Ambrosetown, were by any standards pointless. Brushing away the sillier suggestions one comes to the likely conclusion that map-reading was to blame. The bomber's approach to the substantial creamery used a copybook technique, if a little opportunistically. The use of *Schleichflug* made it clear that both raids were deliberate and against Welsh targets that were presumed tactical.

Nursed on war films, we tend to assume that the ground seen from a plane is clearer than a map and almost as good as a photograph. In fact cloud could obscure and distort vision to a serious extent. Though the raid occurred in fine August sunshine there were many dense white clouds over that part of County Wexford. Most members of German aircrews were under twenty-five years of age and full of exaltation at being able to serve *Führer* and *Vaterland*; the pilots had somehow drifted from their original formation set, perhaps to bomb the steel works at Port Talbot on the south coast of Wales; even fully laden bombers travel very fast and could have covered the fifty miles between St David's Head in Pembrokeshire and Carnsore Point in Wexford in a matter of minutes. All these factors contributed to a minor tragedy that was deliberately played down by the censor in the name of the Irish government. There was an investigation afterwards and during the debriefing it must have become clear that a geographical error had occurred. This may have been the reason that the German authorities made no demur about paying £9000 in reparation in 1944, although it was less than 60% of the original claim.

The causes of the raids of the early days of January 1941 may be more complicated. They were more dramatic in that they included the capital's first taste of aerial bombardment severally in the attacks at Donore Terrace not far from the city centre, Templeogue and on the railway station at Sandycove. They also caused further deaths when bombs off-loaded in County Carlow killed three women. It was probably coincidental that the raids followed closely on the Irish government refusal to allow new German legation staff to be flown in to Rineanna, the forerunner of Shannon Airport, in a civilian plane. They were said to be civilian meteorologists but no one believed this. The general feeling was that the number of officials at 58 Northumberland Road was sufficient for general purposes. Even the very *Hunde* on *Unter den Linden* knew that these extra officials were military attachés but de Valera's refusal to allow even a civilian German plane invade Irish air space was what caused the trouble. The more von Ribbentrop thundered the more adamant de Valera became, in spite of hospitalisation for one of many eye operations. It was made clear that should the German plane, even if civilian, be spotted over Irish territory the ADC's aircraft would attack it, as would any ack-ack guns within range. De Valera won in the end after six days of stand-off, suggesting with forked tongue that there would be no objection to the extra staff being sent by sea, or as he put it 'by ordinary transportation facilities'. In fact there were no ordinary facilities available. No American ships called at Ireland any more, British ships were hardly suitable and what Irish ships there were had by agreement to call at British ports.

The raids, coming so soon after Ribbentrops's diplomatic defeat by de Valera, were thought by the Cabinet to be punitive, especially as Henning Thomsen, Hempel's assistant, strutted a bit as he insisted that the three nights of attacks had been caused by mistakes on the part of inexperienced aircrews who had mistaken Dublin for Liverpool. He ominously warned the government that Ireland had been lucky not to have come under attack more often. Moreover, the perceived Jewishness of some of the targets was regarded as significant. All Dubliners knew well that the area around the South Circular Road was where Dublin Jews tended to live and the fact that their synagogue had been damaged gave the man-in-the street food for some thought and much more conversation. To add to the confusion, the Swastika Laundry continued to allow its vans, now driven by electricity, to sport the adopted Nazi emblem as they made their deliveries.

Even odder was the presence on the uniform edition of the works of Rudyard Kipling (1865–1936), never banned and available in all the city libraries, of the symbol insisted by him to be a Sanskrit token of good fortune. The government again accepted Hempel and Thomsen's assurances that there had never been any intention of bombing any part of Éire and faced down protests about the two trips north that the Dublin fire fighters had made during the severe bombing of Belfast.

It was somewhat ironic that the last bombing of Irish territory should have occurred not in belligerent Belfast but in inner-city Dublin. The events of the night of 30-31 May remain as a trauma for all who experienced them, even now nearly seventy years later. All kinds of explanations were offered for the *real* cause of the raids and it is something of an anti-climax that they too are likely to have been caused by the combination of human error and weather conditions that exculpated German from any real charge of deliberate intention. And so after many charges of flawed neutrality on one side and intentional belligerence on the other, truth, the daughter of time, has shown that with a really good advocate neither charge would stick; no jury would be persuaded to find the defendants guilty.

The existence of the air corridor, the sharing of meteorological information, the difference in treatment between Allied and Axis prisoners of war and perhaps most significantly the removal of any possibility of successful German espionage, all showed that the Irish government, effectively controlled by de Valera, were neutral for the Allies and neutral against the Axis powers. The instant approval of Belfast's requests for fire-fighting help on two occasions could have been taken legally as a breach of any neutrality code since Northern Ireland, (whatever about the feelings of its two-fifths nationalist population) was belligerent and still legally part of the British Empire. De Valera's cool-headed forensic argument and Aiken's more emotional outburst that those in trouble in Belfast were 'our own people' was legalistically if not morally unsound. From the point of view of Germany all the incursions into Irish airspace were caused partly by the accident of bad tracking but mainly because the partially lit counties of Wexford, Wicklow, Dublin Meath and Louth provided a clear pathway to their primary targets in England, Wales, Scotland and, of course, on three scorching occasions Belfast.

The deaths, amounting in total to almost forty – if you count the people who died when the Old Bride Street tenements collapsed the next morning – could in no sense be attributed to individual malice. In counties Wexford and Carlow the fatalities may have been a part of the usual collateral damage that makes civilians in war vulnerable. The bombardier and/or the pilot responsible for the Campile deaths had found what seemed like a prime target. The Knockroe killings happened as a result of standard off-loading of unused bombs on what seemed from the air early on a winter morning a region of open countryside. It was the North Strand bombings early on Whit Saturday that caused the greatest number of casualties, eventually agreed to be thirty-four, with ninety seriously injured, that caused the greatest shock and the greatest fever of speculation as to cause. Some were certain that it was a punishment raid for the help given by the fire fighters in Belfast. Other blamed it on British interference with radio beams; Churchill himself suggested this as a cause. The Air

Corps, partly as an exercise, followed the route of the bombers the following week and found that with the same weather conditions the area was a clearly specified as on a large-scale map. It must, they felt, have been impossible for the pilot not to have known his location. In his important work on the coastal watching service, *Guarding Neutral Ireland* (2008), Michael Kennedy of the Royal Irish Academy has noted that the frequent German flights along the east coast had at this period become so erratic that it was impossible to plot their courses.

The most probable cause was that having failed to discover their assigned targets, the pilots found themselves lost. The correct procedure as dictated by their training was to jettison any disposable cargo, especially since their fuel gauges would by then have been showing low. Dropping this excess would bring about an immediate improvement in flight time because of lesser weight and greater speed. Furthermore, they could fly at a greater and therefore safer height. Other possible factors were navigational error, equipment malfunction and, a significant determining factor, weather. Compared with any other city in these islands, Dublin was hardly scratched. Belfast had more than thirty times the number of fatalities and Liverpool, Coventry, Plymouth, Glasgow, Birmingham, Manchester, Leeds, Sheffield and of course, London, withstood raids, day and night, for most of a year. (We may add 'Hell-Fire Corner', the south-east triangle of Kent, centred on Dover, over which the Battle of Britain was fought and which was subject to continuous shell fire from German coastal batteries in France.) Yet the Dublin deaths, apart from the grief of the victims' families and friends, caused a kind of national, collective trauma. The 'neutral island' had

had its taste of modern warfare and the country very briefly lost confidence in its leaders. A press photograph of the time shows de Valera and Aiken staring dumbfounded into the main crater on North Strand Road.

Opinion soon swung back behind the government because of the sterling performance of the Defence Force system, both professional and voluntary, and because of the acceptance by Germany of responsibility and the promise to pay compensation. The Irish government paid £344,000 to the bereaved and injured and in 1958 accepted £327,000 from the West Germany of the time. The Communist *Deutsche Demokratische Republik*, known then as East Germany, paid nothing and even after the reunification of Germany on 3 October 1990 did not feel any need to accept some of the responsibility. Neither did Austria, though by international law it was part of the *Reich* at the time of the bombing and as such was partly liable for the deaths and destruction caused by the *Luftwaffe*. As if to show that Germany was then at the height of its power and that its interpretation of the concept of neutrality was as subjective as that of Éire's, on 13 June 1941 the Rosslare–Fishguard ferry, *Patrick,* was dive-bombed and sunk by German aircraft a few miles off the Welsh coast. Twenty-three people were lost.

The Dublin bombing, as it still remembered has found its place in childhood memories recalled in print. Edith Newman Devlin recalled both the Belfast blitz and the Dublin one in her memoir, *Speaking Volumes: A Dublin Childhood* (2000). Returning from a trip to Belfast in 1941 she felt glad to be leaving the war behind. She was all the more startled when Clontarf, where she was living to keep her pregnant sister company, was shaken by explosions that seemed very close. They listened to the neighbours, all standing at their doorways wondering aloud if the planes had mistaken them for an English city, then fled to the security of the cupboard under the stairs. About six o'clock the milkman arrived and assured them that 'half of Dublin had been wiped out and hundreds of people killed.'

Peter Somerville Large was at prep school in Laragh House during the Emergency and recalled the experience in his book *Irish Voices* (1999). Referring to the Dublin Blitz he quotes Alex King, the Chief Air Warden as saying that though the whole place was a shambles 'the North Strand people were absolutely out of this world...There was always tea going' – and lots of sandwiches.

The night of 30-31 May 1941 was remembered on 31 May 2001, the sixtieth anniversary of the bombing, when a plaque was unveiled at Charleville Mall public library close to the scene of the North Strand Road deaths. On 31 May 2008, in St Agatha's Church in North William Street, a special service was held to commemorate the sixty-seventh anniversary of what was the most dramatic – and tragic – event in the history of the parish. (The commemoration of the bombing was part of the centenary celebrations of the church, appropriately since it was one of many buildings damaged by the Whitsun bombs.)

Among the congregation that included Bertie Ahern, Aodhan Ó Ríordáin, the Deputy Lord Mayor of the city, other members of the City Council, and representatives of the Garda Síochána, the St John's Ambulance, the Red Cross and Civil Defence, was Sr Martha DC of the Daughters of Charity at Knock. Then in her ninety-first year, she recalled how as a young nun of twenty-two in her convent in North

William Street she helped to care for the injured and homeless.

The service was led by the parish priest Fr Brian Lawless, whose few words reminded his listeners that 'although our country was neutral, it didn't mean that it was immune from attacks during the war. There was no guarantee that Ireland would be untouched by the war.' Invited by the priest, Sister Martha came forward to light a memorial candle. It was right to remember the terrible night (and its generally unsung sequel in Old Bride Street). The candle, symbolic of so many things, was a fitting closure to a dark but heroic episode in the city's history. It may not have been Éire's finest hour but it was a honourable and heroic one.

# Select Bibliography

Brown, Terence. *Ireland: A Social and Cultural History 1922–2002*. London: 2004.

Coogan, Tim Pat. *Ireland in the Twentieth Century*. London: 2003.

Devlin, Edith Newman. *Speaking Volumes: A Dublin Childhood*. Belfast: 2000.

Fanning, Ronan. *Independent Ireland*. Dublin: 1983.

Fisk, Robert. *In Time of War*. London: 1983.

Girvin, Brian. *The Emergency: Neutral Ireland 1939–45*. London: 2006.

Girvin, Brian and Geoffrey Roberts (eds). *Ireland and the Second World War*. Dublin: 2000.

Geraghty, Tom and Trevor Whiteside. *The Dublin Fire Brigade*. Dublin: 2004.

Hickey D.J. and J.E. Doherty. *A New Dictionary of Irish History*. Dublin: 2003.

Kennedy, Michael. *Guarding Neutral Ireland*. Dublin: 2008.

Keogh, Dermot. *Twentieth-Century Ireland*. Dublin: 1994.

Lyons F.S.L. *Ireland since the Famine*. London: 1978.

Nowlan, Kevin B. and T. Desmond Williams (eds.). *Ireland in the War Years and After*. Dublin: 1969.

O'Brien, Mark. *De Valera, Fianna Fáil and the* Irish Press. Dublin: 2001.

-------------------*The Irish Times: A History*. Dublin: 2008.

O'Toole, Fintan. *The Irish Times Book of the Century*. Dublin: 1999.

Patterson, Henry. *Ireland Since 1939*. Oxford: 2002.

Redmond, Sean. *Belfast Is Burning 1941*. Dublin: 2002.

Share, Bernard. *The Emergency: Neutral Ireland: 1939–45*. Dublin: 1978.

Sloan G.R. *The Geopolitics of Anglo-Irish Relations in the Twentieth Century*. London: 1997.

Somerville-Large, Peter. *Irish Voices*. London: 1999.

Townshend, Charles. *Ireland: The Twentieth Century*. London: 1998.

Wills, Clair. *That Neutral Island*. London: 2007.

Wood, Ian S. *Ireland during the Second World War*. London: 2002.